ANATOMY OF A THOUGHT

A Study of human emotions

Rohit Agnihotri

ISBN-13:978-1468145168
ISBN-10:1468145169

DEDICATION

To the eternal memory of

Pandit Hutashan Dev Ji Pandey

With love and respect

For
My loving family

My daughter Aprajita

and my wife Priti

Forever

ACKNOWLEDGMENTS

My parents

Shri Ram Sut Agnihotri &

Dr. Shail Bala

For inculcating in me

the traits of

objective inquiry

and assertive expression

Preface

This document aims to familiarize the readers with innovative ideas at the edge of the human consciousness by employing the technique of looking around the edges.

This treatise essentially aims at bringing to the forefront of cognition what we already know and leverage this to attain targeted results.

This dissertation does assume some prerequisites in terms of well-known concepts and perceptions.

'We, ourselves, have to be the change that we wish to see in the world'

Let us think of re-incarnation as a continuation of the acquired knowledge assimilated into the wisdom within an endless continuum that neither has a defined beginning nor a definite end but extends ad-infinitum in the temporal and spatial perspectives.

Re-incarnation:

Re-incarnation is the perpetuation of evolution of thought through generations.

We are essentially talking about the continual evolution of thought, irrespective of survival of human body in which the thought resides temporarily for a short period; that is, but a fleeting moment in the context of the cosmic awareness and almost infinite time-lines.

"The greater danger, for most of us is not that our aim is too high and we miss it, but that it is too low and we reach it."   *- Michelangelo*

TABLE OF CONTENTS

GENESIS   page 02

EVOLUTION   page 30

Re-incarnation   page 61

ESSENCE   page 72

Reality and perception   page 74

MATURITY   page 93

Truth   page 98

Conscience   page 127

OBLIVION   page 131

Risk and errors   page 144

Glossary   page 146

Bibliography   page 150

Rohit Agnihotri

GENESIS

It all starts with a barely perceptible miniscule burst of energy, in the nether region of the brain called subconscious mind. Latent energy of this phenomenon then enables it to traverse the subconscious mind and bloom in to our awareness, in such a sudden occurrence that more often than not, we are caught unawares.

I seek a parallel for this phenomenon in creation of the universe that started with a brief flash of light, the pure energy, which then blossomed into an all-enveloping occurrence that resulted in the creation of mass, which led to the existence of the universe as we know it today.

When this spontaneous sparkle, which is pure energy, reaches the realms of cognizance, the conscious mind or active awareness region, whether it fizzles out in ignominy or brightens the horizon with a great burst of coruscation, depends entirely on the associations it attracts and also the bonds it forms with the other cognizable thought forms.

These preexisting thought patterns sustain the diminishing energy of the brief sparkle of the burgeoning idea and help it to blossom into a full-fledged thought that forms contiguous bonds with preexisting cognitive content, to entrench itself in the relevant thought spectrum.

Thoughts are the purest form of instant energy, which are liberating by nature and coax the reorganization of the thought map in a fascinating array of relevant thought forms that tumble upon each other in a roller coaster ride that prides itself on its reluctant execution of the full loop, which enables turning the thought forms upside down to test their mettle to weed out trivial from significant.

This is a practical exposition of Darwin's theory of 'survival of the fittest' in an unrelenting maneuver. It is the recognition of what we know (Meta-knowledge) and what we know not, that elevates the human existence above other life forms on the planet earth.

Actually, it is far more important to understand as to what we seek, what we want to know and why. This approach carefully sculpts the thought-scape and defines the boundaries of what we need to know.

The need to know sounds very final and we must deliberately eschew these definite limits and continue to test the preset boundaries for their veracity and currency in the ever-changing environ. Another method, which is available to us, is to target exclusion of, what we do not need to know.

Since, there are fewer members in this set; this exercise may prove to be very helpful in excluding what we do not need to know, to arrive at what we need to know. This indeed is simpler but still remains an exacting task that we have set for ourselves. We also need to be aware of, at all times that the available knowledge base is an ever expanding set and the new items that get added with frustrating regularity, need to be continually examined for relevance, addressed and cataloged, as required.

I have touched upon the thought associations and now we need to delve deeper into this phenomenon to understand its true nature and implications. We humans are endowed with powerful abilities of associative memory and Meta-knowledge.

Associative memory can be defined as the phenomenon of one thing reminding us of another, leading to a comprehensive thought relationship mapping. Meta-knowledge deals with knowledge about knowledge and provides us with useful pointers to the relevant item of the knowledge that we seek assiduously.

For example, if I were to ask you, if you know your residence phone number, you are likely to answer with an instant 'yes'. However, if I ask you that if you know the date of birth of Albert Einstein; you may answer 'no'. The issue under discussion is, as to how we instantly know what we know and what we know not and why we do not have to think long and hard to arrive at the answer.

It is this trait of Meta-knowledge that allows us to instantly recognize as to what we know and what we do not. Sometimes, the Meta-knowledge becomes more important than the knowledge itself.

This labyrinth of interconnected facts helps us to form an idea that develops in to a full-fledged thought. This remains locked in the maze, till we tap it for practical application. This association is the genesis of thought, which delivers us from the confusion and is also the key to the logic of the birth of thought that renders useless our efforts to gain an insight in to the birth of thought, as it is happening here and now, right in front of our eyes.

Many a time, importance of several steps in this phenomenon may escape us, for we take a lot of things for granted, such as the sunrise and the sunset and for the young people, flipping of a switch to put on the light.

Thoughts have expiry dates and in case of replication, we will do well to check the current validity before re-application of the thought and our launching in to action. At times, this spontaneous burst of activity can lead to an unsuccessful endeavor, due to lack of preparation.

Depending upon expected need of use in the temporal perspective, the thought is stored in multiple level memory storage of the mind having different access times, with a purpose of optimal utilization of the resources. The conscious mind is like the computer RAM (Random Access Memory) with very fast access time.

The subconscious mind is akin to the hard disk type of secondary memory storage with significantly higher access time. Some things like values and the elegance of social interaction are etched upon our mind, once only, by the society, parents and the teachers and this can be compared to the ROM (Read Only Memory).

A thought does not exist in a vacuum, but in a crowded relational space that gives it the associative embrace of significance, which is another crowded space called emotions. The very perception of relevance of the thought or otherwise gives it the position of eminence or shoves it beyond oblivion.

When we decide to banish a thought, it does not get erased entirely but is kept stored in the trash folder that resides in our subconscious mind. This thought then remains in hibernation, till the time it is needed again and then it gets propelled in to the awareness domain as a hunch, in the time of need.

Sometimes, these hunches provide the much needed solution pointers that otherwise elude us, as we are busy with direct thinking and do not wish to be side tracked.

A good idea, in the form of a hunch, knocks at the hallowed portals requesting for admittance; Once, twice, again and yet again. We get irritated and shout 'go away'. The thought goes away; puzzling, is it not?

How can it go away when we needed it the most? All of them are Traitors. Once we are able to think of thoughts as people, we get accustomed to their need for recognition and pampering without which they tend to wither away, if their ego has been hurt.

Each thought is based upon hundreds of ideas that owe their origin to infinite number of subliminal impulses that the labyrinth of intertwined connectivity of the thought forms provides to us, as minute bursts of contained energy that are the basic first level inputs to the intricate thought building process.

The relentless expedition to seek and collate all related information that is needed to formulate a thought, is a continual activity that happens incessantly in our brain without our being fully aware of it, most of the time.

The extraordinary bandwidth of this information super highway has always been a challenge to the scientists in the IT domain, who have tried to create an artificial model for the same; to be used for quick information retrieval and working out of the relevant associations in the realm of gigantic information storage, spanning the entire world.

When we get into the discussion on the anatomy of thought, it surely will gravitate to the thought inhibitors also. Our inhibitions, impressions and learning are the major thought inhibitors along with the social upbringing that is product of the times and society we exist in. For example, many vegetarians, self-included, will not even think of consuming meat and if the thought at all forms due to external suggestions in the form of peer pressure, the thought inhibitors are enabled instantly.

These strong thought inhibitors that have their origin in our upbringing and value system will be strongly activated to cancel the thought and also put a stigma against it for future proscription of origin of any such thought.

In the same way, a teenager brought up in a strict conservative family will shun casual sex, even though it is a primeval craving and also a serious contender for peer pressure example. Our training of inhibitors starts immediately upon being born and brought in to the world.

All our feelings, experiences and learning acquired through childhood and teen age are part of the intellectual make-up that governs our behavior all through life. At this stage, effects of the subliminal impulses are highest and these inputs condition and shape our mind in such a manner that these shall determine our responses, all through our life. A baby, who is not breast-fed, will never learn to appreciate the true warmth of relationships. I agree that this is an unfair example and later interactions and associations will help inculcate the required basics but intensity of the emotion may have been permanently impaired.

Please note that this isolated example is in no way indicative of the influence on all future interactions but it may cause an effect nevertheless. Infants have a lot of curiosity and many a time loving parents tend to curb it with a barrage of admonitions. This act, though required to keep the infant away from danger, has an undesirable side to it. This course of action will instill an inhibition in the young person against curiosity.

A chain of logical thought in the mind of the child has been curbed in favor of security and experimentation is prohibited. A child needs to experiment. Though, the parent is correct about keeping experimentation within the bounds of safety, it would be better, if it is explained to the child, as to why certain things are not to be attempted, with a stress on the danger and need for safety.

It is not necessary, that all the reasoning has to be fully understood by the child; what is more important is to expose the child to the mode of explanation and understanding that in itself is a reassuring feeling, even for the adults.

The advent of teenage brings the discussion to the taboo subject of sex. The physiological changes in the human body at this age are of great concern to young people. The feelings of curiosity and experimentation are strongest at this age and need to be addressed with detailed explanations that must include expressions of veracity. If the young people do not have access to the information, they may seek the same from less appropriate or even inappropriate sources.

The early impressions may also influence the probability of my answering the teacher's question in a class, if I only know part of the answer. In fact, these early inputs will compromise the effectiveness of our action even if we know the full and correct answer.

These early impressions, inhibitions and influences form the basis of the persuasions that will guide our behavior all though life, because our mind was at the most impressionable stage at this time. Then, there are impressions that we form about people.

Young people have close friends and best friends. Ever thought as to why adults only have friends and lovers? No best friends anymore. At this highly impressionable teen age, young people tend to hang around with the crowd that comprises like-minded people, who may have had a lot of piercings and may have experimentation as their life blood. They are part of the "been there-done that" crowd you want your youngster to stay away from.

Me and my child had similar if not the same upbringing and if this is the main influence on thoughts, how come my kid does not dislike what I dislike?

Ask that question in the changed format; how come I do not like what my offspring likes so much? Here, we are forgetting other thought influences like the times, we live in. Upbringing may be the same but external influences have changed a lot. Peer pressure makes the teenagers like loud, rambunctious music even if they have been raised on the solid diet of classical music. This works same way for clothing and hair also.

The doyens of fashion decide what is nice and what is out of favor. Today, even preteens are so very conscious about apparel selection and make-up and any attempt to enforce a rationale favored by adults in the household is likely to be met with lot of resistance and even rebellion.

Peer pressure, not only is a serious influence on thoughts but more often than not, may be the genesis of many a thought that would not have raised their heads otherwise, against heavy fortifications of well-established family values and conservative upbringing.

Now that we have dwelt upon the topic of genesis of thought sufficiently enough for a sound foundation, I offer to introduce classification of thoughts that actually lends itself to multiple criteria and I shall recognize and address some of these in the ensuing discussion.

We shall include some examples that pursue a line of thought for the uninitiated to get a grasp of the discourse.

A colorful robin streaks across the sky allowing us a brief look that we may classify as a glance at this time and we think what a beautiful bird. This is a fleeting thought.

Then the time stamp changes and we can only say that a beautiful bird flew by. This is retained image of the thought. In another example a beautiful girl walks past us and we think that she is a beautiful girl. This is a considered thought as we are comparing the visage of the girl with other good looking people we know and can think of; at this moment. This comparison trait or discerning ability helps us in evaluation of overlapping alternatives.

Next, I take up an example of the rainbow. I know from prior experience that a rainbow is mostly visible when the sun shines just after a rain shower and there is high moisture content in the atmosphere. It is at this time, when I shall call my daughter outside to have her witness formation of the rainbow. This is an experienced thought that leads to a considered action.

Moving forward, we come to an example, which we shall use for several scenarios and targeted inferences. This example is that of a precariously balanced nest of a little bird nestled in the crook of the fork, in a branch high up in a majestic tree. The nest is busily resounding with cries of a gaggle of the young, recently hatched chicks. The mother bird comes back with a couple of tasty looking worms and cuts them up in small morsels before offering them to chicks. This is an example of the developed thought.

The mother bird, either by its own experience or close observation of other mother birds, experienced in this endeavor, knows that young chicks can handle only small morsels and accordingly adjusts the food offering to make it suitable for the tiny receivers of the food.

Another scenario is with the same stage setting. A large snake is crawling up the tree towards the nest probably with an intention of gobbling up the chicks. The mother bird almost by intuition recognizes this nefarious intent and attacks the snake. This is an action born out of the interpreted thought based on earlier experience and/ or observation. Actually, there is another thought process going on simultaneously which I expected to take up later.

The example is here and the associated interpretation is staring us in the face and being the righteous people that we are, we cannot walk away from the obvious and the demand of time, in which we operate and live in, minute by minute and second by second.

It is a big snake and any attempt to kill it or even scare it away is far too onerous a task for the small mother bird, so as to be almost suicidal in nature, because due to disparity in size, the snake may actually end up swallowing the mother bird. It is not that the mother bird is unaware of consequences of this reckless action on her part. So why does the mother bird even attempt it?

Answer to this, lies in the definition of the most basic need of all living beings, which is a continual and consistent effort towards perpetuation of our race in general and that of the immediate family lineage in particular.

Why do we even help another person? The genesis of this thought, which is motivation for this act, irrespective of countless invocations of altruism, is actually very plain and simple. The act of helping someone is with a built-in expectation that the other person will help us in our time of need, when our need for help may be even higher than that of the other person being helped by us, at this time.

Let us add another dimension to it. Power of thought is simply incalculable. Many a time, I know, or at least think and believe that, the person being helped by me at this time is never going to be in a position to be able to offer any tangible help to me, now or later. So we look for another justification.

It is in our basic human nature, as an ingrained quality, to help someone in need. We actually do not need any justification but expression of the same, seems to help the external manifestation.

So, extension into another dimension is such that, when I help someone, who helps someone, who helps someone else, this perpetual chain of individual help efforts, helps to connect together the humanity and sustain it.

The possibility that one of these people, helped by this sustained chain of help started by me, may at some point of time help me or my progeny is not even a shadow at the most distant horizon, but still this possibility at the basic level is a primeval force of the universe that binds us, keeps us together and protects us.

This further develops into a thought that provides the base for the often quoted expression, 'the greatest good for the greatest number of people.'

This is the sustaining force and also the driving argument, which is the cause of people giving up their lives, for the greatest good for the society and the Nation.

Now that we are in the territory of thoughts and emotions, please do let me mention bravery, which is quite misunderstood, at times. A person jumps in to action in a battle, in the face of certain death and achieves martyrdom, without even knowing the danger or understanding the possible impact of it.

I would class this as a foolhardy action on part of the individual, fit only for the postscript as the heartless statistics that converts a living person into a numeric addition to the total number of heroic dead in action.

One, who is not aware of the danger, performs an act of impulse and not of bravery

Then, there are other individuals who know and understand the danger to their own life but launch in to action, which is the thing to be done in alignment with the demand of situation and circumstances faced by them to serve the need, even at the highly probable risk of laying down their own life, to achieve the stated objective of the greatest good for the greatest number of people.

Now, these indeed are the people worthy of all the eulogies and then some.

 Next item that catches my fancy and therefore requires your committed attention is that of our thought and resultant action of helping kith and kin.

My progeny gets to a good station in life with my help and they will most likely help me in turn when I am old, frail, infirm and in need of help. This now is too direct to bring in selflessness but direct things have the benefit of a ring of truth and are useful for this trait and the exhibition of it.

I also have a need for you to believe in my assertions and it is this relentless craving that forces me to go into detailed discussion on the topic and timely insertion of relevant examples.

My dear captive audience, if you thought that I might have lost the thread of discussion after several of these side steps, if not digression, you have a second thought coming.

It takes much more than this to put me off the continuation; but yes, this indeed has been somewhat heavy discussion and I do think that you may have earned a well-deserved respite. Okay, I cannot be too generous on this, but please do take a short break, while I collect my ideas on the derived thought to continue further.

Someone, who is fully aware of the danger in a certain enterprise but attempts it nevertheless, because this is an endeavor for realizing the greatest good for the greatest number of people, indeed performs an act of bravery and should be rightfully called a hero.

Our resolve and tenacity is greater than our fears and this enables us to undertake a demanding journey beyond the limits of our fortitude. Our courage, in the face of known consequences, is our guiding light; which is our beacon and the source of our strength.

We shall now take up an example of a series of laboratory experiments and see as to how this fits the spectrum, which we have carefully woven with complex opinions and simple relational linkages to connect it up.

Gregor Johann Mendel (1822 – 1884)

Gregor Johann Mendel, is known as the "father of modern genetics", born: July20, 1822 Heinzendorf bei Odrau, Austrian Empire, current Czech Republic.

We take the inferences of individual experiments and connect them up to derive a probable hypothesis, which has to be tested against still more stringent parameters. It was such a series of seemingly uncorrelated experiments, inferences from which, connected together by logical threads and a common theme resulted in the development of the theory of genetics by Gregor Johann Mendel.

The next category of classification that we take up is direct and implied thoughts. Direct thought, as the nomenclature clearly signifies is our first impression or our first-cut thoughts on the issue or situation.

Here, we shall lean on the study of psychology to show us the way. Let us take up the Rorschach test. This is popularly known as the ink-blot test. The irregular ink-blot that does not signify anything through verifiable observation is shown to the subject (individual attempting the test) and the person is asked to recognize or at least put a near identity to the asymmetrical ink-blot graphic.

In our example study, the subject (the person being subjected to the thought analysis) identifies the irregular ink blot shape as a 'thumbs-up sign'. This is a direct thought. The implied thought here is that the subject is looking at approval. This can also mean a signal for going ahead in a derived perspective. Now, this is an aberration; what is a member of another classification doing here? This was supposed to be taken up later.

The derived thought is that all these classification scenarios are not standalone entities with clear boundaries, but in reality these classified sets are both overlapping and interrelated. The overlapping scenario may sound incompetent but actually is a very important tool, of which we must take cognizance, for developing associations that assist the evolution and maintenance of Meta-knowledge.

Now we come to an individual's thought and a group's thought. The thought of a group is an idea that has been discussed and on which group consensus has been achieved. Needless to say, but let us state anyway that the group thought is inherently more powerful, refined and better stated.

Then, there is a thought that is lurking in the background patiently, waiting for recognition and for being called to the forefront. This type of thought essentially feeds on derived power of accumulated information, commonly referred to as a hunch. When this moves to the discernible domain, it changes character, as now we have a plethora of thoughts and information available, to help build and support its veracity. All sensory input is raw data. It becomes information when we are able to categorize and catalog it. This information moves another step forward to earn the knowledge label, when the perspective tag along with analytical inferences is added to this entity.

The final stage of transformation is achieved when the thought is streamlined and shaped, so as to be able to support replication in the similar intended environment or even in a different setting, though still retaining the associated spatial and temporal flags. We have seen transformation of thought from larvae state to a beautiful butterfly that sprouting of wings and taking to air signifies and finally free from the earthbound characteristics, the thought blooms and comes of age in a splash of rainbow colors and much more important, with a new upgraded aim of the sky.

The next classification category we target is subdued and assertive thought. The subdued thought lacks confidence in itself and tries to seek support of other powerful and/ or proven thoughts, whereas assertive thought is a confident standalone entity; which, if need be, can imbue the confidence, even in its vehicle thought, in an unlikely probability that it should need one. This assertive thought can carry another, which may need the support.

Next category is well-crafted vs. hastily assembled thought. Let us look at some examples here:

"He has all the virtues I dislike and none of the vices I admire." - Winston Churchill

"A modest little person, with much to be modest about." -Winston Churchill

"I apologize for the length of this letter but I didn't have the time to make it shorter." – Mark Twain

"I have never killed a man, but I have read many obituaries with great pleasure." -Clarence Darrow

Now the show stopper:

"The greatest challenge to any thinker is stating the problem in a way that will allow a solution." - Bertrand Russell

Please do forgive me for not being able to give an example of poorly crafted thought as I do not collect rubbish. I know that my efficient detractors; I seem to be able to collect those at will, well respected by me, will seize this opportunity with alacrity to gleefully comment that other than these quotations rest of the book is a good example of poorly crafted thoughts and since I am feeling quite generous right now, I may allow the devil its due.

Moving on, let us now talk about positive and negative thoughts. Please note that both of these are very strong contenders, when we come to think of the effectiveness with which these thoughts hold court and rule absolutely.

Positive thoughts envelop us and give us power of sustenance that in the beginning, we may not have thought possible. The antonym face of negative thoughts saps our energy, inculcates lethargy and acceptance of vagaries of life, by simply giving in.

This capitulation occurs without our putting up even a semblance of fight, as our discharged energy levels do not permit a struggle, which would have established our credentials in the domain and among our peers, as the group of confident people, capable of supporting our deeply held belief and expressed thought.

So what do we do? Give up, pack our bags and go home? There was a time, long, long ago, when I was a lot younger; yes, I actually was young once, though even to me this sounds something far too distant.

Hey, all you good looking people out there, I am not all that ancient; it is only that, when I start thinking on the issues being pondered upon here, I do not feel very young.

So, where is the positive thought? When people check with me as to how old I am, I respond with a tongue in cheek reply, ' I am fifty one years young.'

I hope, everyone will agree to accept and acknowledge this as a positive statement. We hope for and target what we can do, but in life's arrangement of events, our hopes do not always come true. I do hear a voice of dissonance indicating that this offering is not enough. So here is another:

When I get asked as to what is my outlook on life; I reply with a simple well-crafted response, rehearsed well in advance. Okay, well-crafted in my opinion, for whatever my opinion may be worth.

My outlook of life and my blood group are the same, **B+**

Be Positive; this detail is just for those impersonators, who masquerade as my audience; if you still do not get it. If someone still does not think this to be a statement positive enough, you have to wait for my next book that shall be named 'philosophy for dummies'.

Sorry paying customers, but sometimes it pays to be rude, if you are able to achieve the effect that such an action is your birthright. It is all about confidence actually, is it not? So, when I was young, once upon a time; long, long ago, I inquired of a girl, a work place colleague of mine, whose presence I could feel just by instinct; do you think I have a chance or should I pack my bags and go home?

Till date, I do not know whether she declined or did not get it, at all. We just parted without a word and then went on with our respective lives. This is not very assertive surely. Was I thinking positive? Not really.

Intelligent people learn from their mistakes. Wise people learn from mistakes of others. You decide, what category do you belong to and more important actually, as to which category do you wish to belong to now.

If I can only manage to get you to shift your aim to be in the group of the wise, then I have succeeded in my endeavor that I targeted by writing this volume, and you would have definitely achieved value for the money, you have invested in buying this book.

Another term that is the sibling of "value" is "worth". What is the worth of our work? Worth of our work is only as much as the minimum amount of money, using which, the same amount and same quality of work can be achieved, as the amount and quality of work accomplished by us. Sometimes this can be a very revealing, scary and also demeaning exercise. So, I suggest that you may choose not to indulge in this exercise, unless it is imperative and even then, I suggest that we give it some thought before embarking upon such a humbling endeavor.

I do not target lofty aims, nor do I settle for within reach targets. The trick is to set stretch targets for ourselves that require stretching ourselves to the limit, to be actualized. Sometimes, we are not aware of our own hidden strengths and the high degree of potential energy that resides within us. These are times when we need a friend, another human being, with an ability of objective assessment of our abilities in a detached sort of way. Someone, who reminds us of our abilities and exhorts us to bring them to fore, to tackle the job at hand and accomplish it with the excellence expected of us.

Some of us, perhaps many of us, harbor this incorrect notion that thoughts are free roaming entities, which necessarily need to live up to their nomadic existence by continuously traversing entire canvas of the thought-scape, of which they are only a transient member.

It may be accepted that thoughts are wandering entities which move on the continuously moving ticker tape of time, until they are plucked out of there by a mind that is urgently seeking them.

Thoughts are like a new-born baby that may seem to be without any linkages, but if truth be known, the thoughts as well as new-born babies, even before they are conceptualized, begin to almost actually exist in an environment that is waiting for them with open arms and welcomes them to take their rightful place in the optimal relational space, already formed with necessary linkages, which is replete with associations such as parent-child, sibling kinship, grandparent-grandchild relationship and the umpteen cousin connections, which already exist.

Similarly, thoughts may also seem to be falling in to carefully woven patterns waiting with open linkages, as if waiting for just this thought to occur. Many a time, a new thought is born out of a need to fill the created gap that represents an opportunity linked to a need or requirement, which time presents to us with irritating regularity and exhorts us to address the same.

Genesis of thought is linked closely with strong emotions such as, desire, need, love, lust, pride, conceit, anger, jealousy, repugnance, horror, fear, and desire for fame.

I may not touch upon all of these and definitely not in a sequence or any logical order; I shall indeed address the important entities here and some of these in coherent groups.

The difference between desire and need is indeed simple, as to what we long for, wish or want to have, is desire and need is, what we must have for the purpose of addressing the essential requirement of our continued existence as a participating and contributing entity.

Another set is pride and conceit. Difference between the two is that of degree and attitude that drives the emotion. Whereas pride is just and includes some measure of humbleness intrinsically, conceit is a high degree of self-love that is completely without the humility and bereft of any kind emotion that makes the pride lovable and hence is mostly responded with hatred, and sometimes, even with abhorrence in a uncontrolled manner that it justifiably deserves.

Anger is an outcome of unfulfilled desires. Sometimes, when necessary effort is missing for fulfillment of the desire; this anger is unjustified, but this still is quite a strong emotion and it is staring us in the face, expecting to get requited, satisfied and given its due.

It may be termed unfair, but when it is offspring of jealousy, this powerful emotion must be treated with kid gloves because it has stored within it, the latent energy, which if unleashed, threatens to play havoc with the general scheme of things and morale of individual and the group.

Fear is another strong emotion that may enable us with sustained energy flows to work out a tenable alternative at one hand and on the other hand it may crush our resolve to such an extent, from where, even the legendary phoenix would not be able to engineer a rebirth.

Next, let us talk of fame. This very directly relates to the measure of our status among fellow human beings, who form the social environment, where a cornucopia of other lesser thought points may sternly demand our attention at all times and force us to get into a prioritization exercise for which we may not be ready. However, we need to acknowledge the value of prioritization, which enables us to allocate necessary time for the essential issues.

Respect and honor are consequential offshoots of this. I think we should also consider the probability that renown and regard may be integral to fame rather than being a consequence of it. Love and lust also form part of this spectrum. While love is a positive emotion, lust is an uncontrolled and probably uncontrollable desire that does not even demand its share but simply takes away the object of desire by commandeering it in a no nonsense manner, which is sheer dictatorial aggression.

This point in time requires us to address the thoughts of horror and repugnance. Revulsion is an emotion that we feel when we encounter something, which we do not wish to come in contact with or even see. Repugnance is a feeling that is very strong. For example, we happen to come across the loathsome spectacle of a vulture crawling inside the torso of a bovine carcass with a purpose of devouring the entrails.

The feeling most likely to catch hold of us would be disgust. The horror that we feel looking at such a nauseating spectacle is the consequence of this sickening display. Another face of horror is associated with fear.

For some people being alone in the dark is enough to trigger the fear emotion. The threshold of fear trigger varies in degree from person to person.

However, when this trigger is enabled, the world becomes a scary place. This face of horror feeds on the unexpected, unforeseen and unpredictable. This is the basic recipe that is doled out to us in good measure by producers of horror movies.

Now, here is an interesting point involved; if I am scared of something, why would I want to face it? If that was 100% accurate, makers of horror movies would be out of business. So, what is it? Why do people go to see a horror movie, if it only promises to scare us? This is something that we would wish to avoid under normal circumstances.

The driving urge here is to test the limit of our courage and push it beyond the existing mark. Risk taking is an integral part of the show-off that we undertake to impress the most eligible specimen of opposite gender with a hope that, now well-impressed by the display of our courage, we may get a chance to engage in recreational activities, aiming at procreation with suitably-impressed, outstanding members of the opposite gender of the onlooker group. All the risky and dangerous sports earn good money from the expression and recognition of this single powerful emotion of fear.

Horror has another facet and is quite useful to the living beings in this interpretation. We feel repugnance, when we come to know about the concentration camps of Dachau and other such places, operated by Nazi Germany.

The horrors perpetrated upon the people, incarcerated in these camps, imbue us with such a despicable feeling of hatred that we take a vow to ensure that, such atrocities are never brought upon any other people, irrespective of their political and/ or religious affiliations and cast or creed.

We now see that even the despised feeling of hatred is useful in this specific context. This example may not fit every scenario, but it is only such exceptional occurrences that force the intended outcome of all of us coming together to banish the possibility of any such future recurrence.

This powerful feeling helps us to decide as to what must be ostracized by the society and this very strong feeling of deep-rooted hatred helps to align the people and brings us together against this ugly sentiment, to raise our combined voice for the cause, all of us believe in.

This alignment makes sure that no effort is spared to achieve this goal of banishing all such nauseating, horrendous acts and also the doctrine that promotes these, from the fabric of the society we exist in, by eradicating it in an effective and comprehensive manner.

We do not wish to see or hear of acts such as these anytime in future, irrespective of any degree of dire circumstances that may demand an encore of the same.

Now, let me try to sum up as if we are at the end of the narrative, which we are not, but at the same time this part is a whole in itself and hence deserves a summary. The good part about summarizing is that I am allowed to leave out irritant nuances and annoying constructs that I shall label unworthy.

Please take a note that this labeling only permits us to defer the inevitable and I shall have to address these irritants long before I am through with this thought construct. What is worthy and what is unworthy and in which perspective this is to be judged? Who will be assigned the burdensome responsibility of this task?

I fully understand that I do not measure up to this onerous responsibility. Emotions are the root cause and genesis of thoughts. Strong emotions lead to strong thoughts.

The social training and infusion of values, which inculcate in us, the judgment of right and wrong, provide us with a sustainable perspective. We need to look at thoughts from a dissociated point of view that may be inimical to some of our friends, who choose to interpret thoughts in their own perspective. Since, individual perspectives tend to vary; we are likely to end up with a disparate set of inputs, which may even be in conflict with one another.

These heterogeneous thoughts may even include very basic entities such as values, which are field proven beliefs. The purpose of this interpretation exercise is to include prejudices that we lean upon for deriving inferences suitable to our current frame of psyche.

EVOLUTION

Wait a minute. We are supposed to talk about anatomy of thought and not evolution of it. The essential point here is that these two are intertwined. The dilemma is whether we wish to dissect a live thought or just be content to perform autopsy on the dead ones?

A dead thought is useless. It has no character. It has no discernible form. Now, having said that, I also need to emphasize that a live thought must not die under the scalpel just to ascertain as to what makes it tick. It would be akin to tearing off petal after petal from a rose to come to a conclusion that, as each petal is beautiful, so is the rose; a defeatist scenario indeed.

In this scenario, how do we go about finding anatomy of the thought? We assume that the thought is a black box. Then we give it a standard input and view the output. Observation and analysis of the output with reference to the standard input will enable us to work on a comparable model, which emulates the behavioral pattern of the thought, as it provides the same output when subjected to the standard input.

Now we can tear open the model to look at the innards and try to visualize as to how it works. Let us take the feeling of jealousy as output and give it an input of something that we covet, being achieved by another person. Now when we open the box we find that what we yearn for is always something that has been denied to us but in our opinion we feel that, we are no less deserving than the other person who is receiving accolades on stage. This is the origin of jealousy.

Origin of this thought of jealousy may have a root cause, in the apparent self-denial also, in this perspective.

The core when opened up shows us that it is our ego that has got hurt and has become insatiable. This is a clear case of low self-esteem, which is typical of under achievers. Thoughts have a strong focus on desire and most irrational thoughts, actually have a basis of desire.

So what is desire? What is its foot print? At this time we again lean back on the associations. We do not desire something that we do not know. It all starts with the thought. This is the universal rule.

Sometimes, to explain something complex, we may have to use the entity itself that is under consideration. With the permission of my learned audience, I shall proceed to explain the thought starting with thought itself. We think of a subject.

This subject could be a topic or it could also be an object or a person. When we think of a subject, we get interested in it. Then we try to get in contact with the subject of interest. This contact develops in to the association and we end up forming strong bonds with it.

It is this association that fuels the desire and makes it rampant. Desire is a very strong emotion, fulfillment of which provides satisfaction and the non-achievement may give rise to the feeling of anger.

Anger is not just another strong sentiment, but also a thought that has its origin in the deadly sin of desire, which we have already established to be one of the strongest and most basic of the emotions. Anger, though being a very open emotional state, also is a silent crusader that erodes the very sustenance of the ego and in its angry hunger chomps away the basic tenets of our beliefs.

This leads us to temptation and then to the resultant emotion of infatuation. We like something but the feeling may not be very strong or long-lived. However, if we are denied the object or prohibited from doing something that we very much want to do, this gives genesis to infatuation. Infatuation, the granddaddy of desire, can cause willful destruction of logic and reason. This pathetic state can only go forward to the annihilation of intelligence and devoid of intelligence; a human being is, all but dead.

This very straight path of thinking - association - desire - denial - anger - loss of reason - destruction of intelligence - death is so assured in its absolute certainty that it is almost hypnotic and once in the grip of even the outer fringes of the whirlpool, there is no escape.

Only those, who know, what they do not know, are the people, who may be able to battle their way out of this miasma. The most organized thoughts are those, which are related to our work. Work is too ambiguous a word so I shall narrow it down to the call or the sense of duty.

I am already feeling better. When the thought is focused on the sense of duty, at least we have one of the parameters, the input, in the comprehensible range.

Output may still vary but it is certain that we will be able to define the output also, in the format of a range. This may not be the optimal solution but it can serve the purpose to an acceptable degree at this time.

Shrimad Bhagwad Gita, the holy book of Hindu faith, proclaims that we should only concern ourselves with the action, which is in our domain and we should concentrate all our energy and put to work, our entire ability in a comprehensive manner for executing the task at hand.

This approach targets the task that we have set out to accomplish or the task that has been assigned to us, which is our duty, our responsibility and also our prerogative. When we address these onerous issues, we must keep perspective of the assigned duty. The holy text advises against the possibility of forming a bond with the work that we have set out to do and the outcome.

It asks us to shun any association or desire in relation to the outcome and discard forthwith, all the feeling of any expectation that may have encroached upon our thoughts and can compromise our effort.

One method of approaching this is to concentrate on the work to be done. This is the work that has been identified to be worth being done in alignment with our assertions stated earlier. We must do the assigned work well and when the work is completed to our own satisfaction, we must dissociate ourselves from the outcome and also the consequences like a neutral bystander and refrain from acknowledging the accolades of success as well as the guilt, if the outcome is not to our satisfaction.

The trick is to just observe the happenings with an objective point of view of the spectator watching a game where she/ he does not have her/ his favorite team participating. This much advocated distancing from the final result (A revered Hindu philosophy concept) allows us to objectively view the outcome and build on the positive actions and learn from our mistakes, if called for.

There is a rider here that we must not be in a hurry to proclaim a win, or accept a loss at the outset. This must be put to the ultimate test of time, so that our learning from both win and loss is ingrained in our mind and shall guide future actions with higher levels of certainty and confidence that shall serve us better in the future.

It is the future, for which we are preparing ourselves with concerted effort. We must also be careful not to get in to the trap of accepting **inaction** as a valid option.

According to the holy text even the thought of a thought is reprehensible as it may assume an association. We are advised not to have or feel any association with the work even when we are doing it. This state of dissociation may not be easy to achieve and may require special effort.

We also need to consider the possibility that we may not be capable of this effort, as this requires, not only an understanding of the perspective but may also call upon the practitioner to possess the resolve and ability to let go off the credit that people may consider to be their birthright. If we manage to do something well, it is God's wish and we do not seek any credit for it as it is an outcome of God's wish and design, working through us, using us as a worthy instrument.

At the same time if we commit an error, then again this pattern of thought is helpful as this dissociation also makes us free from any burden of guilt for whatever is happening around or even within, with and/ or by me, is part of the grand design of God and who am I to try to question or even try to decipher and understand the aim and purpose of the doings of God?

We are only the instruments of God

We act in the ways as planned and orchestrated in the overall scheme of events by the Supreme Being with an aim of the greatest good for the greatest number of people. This assumption, at one stroke, makes us free from any guilt or grandeur associations.

Whatever great, good, bad or ugly happens through us, we only watch as an external spectator. This state is quite difficult to achieve for reasons stated hereafter.

I am an integral part of the spectacle presented by ongoing events around us, so how do I dissociate myself from something, of which I am an integral part?

This question has tested the mettle of greatest thinkers of all time. The ultimate aim is to achieve a state of thoughtlessness so perfect that this doctrine of ostracizing all thought, does not even allow us to think about thoughtlessness.

We, benign life forms with ability to think, are only a temporarily segregated iota of the singularity with a focused aim to rejoin with it.

We have established in the above discussion that everything originates from the thought and the thought itself originates from the divine singularity that cannot be described, as expression of it demands an absence of thought. It is to be noted here that the term used here is 'singularity' and not 'one' because the number one may have an attached thought leading to an obscure implication of a possibility of the existence of multiplicity.

Our thoughts are products of our impressions and experiences. Any and every new input is likely to be viewed in the perspective of these paradigms.

Our prejudices shape our thoughts and the individual ego, very subliminally influences the thought process. The much awaited event in our context indeed is transformation of the individual ego to the collective ego as an all-encompassing entity.

This metamorphosis, at a single stroke does away with limitations and highly confounding and confining self-imposed boundaries of the individual ego. This altered focus and the paradigm shift, allows the fruition of our concerted efforts, in the much awaited transmogrification, in the fulfilling form of the much sought after collective ego.

Collective ego is immensely powerful and releases such explosive energy that even the constituents may be excused for holding their collective breath, which an instant later releases in the catharsis of an explosive war cry that astounds the peers and confounds opponents to frustrate them beyond action ability.

Let us get in to the thick of the discussion by taking a closer look at the origin of thought from another perspective. What is the objective of a thought? Quintessential purpose of the thought stares at us and looks for recognition and definition. This is the archetypal need of the perspective that we have chosen to delve into. We hypothesize that all thought is essentially based on the premise that is existence centric.

We need to take the example of an infant, who represents a mind free of unnecessary clutter, beliefs and bias. Here, the thoughts are primarily about hunger, thirst and excretion. All basic needs aimed at preservation of self. Now we grow to the teen age, which is full of conflict, contradictions and peer- pressure. It is here that we learn about assertion and manipulation and not much later, as may be held by popular belief.

You see these at home, classroom, playground, and in the inviting and waiting arms of the big bad wolf; which is the world of a teenager.

The game of who convinces whom goes on and on relentlessly. An unprepared with guile and often defenseless young mind, is striving to keep the head above water, just barely managing to exist.

The next set of deafening questions are already raising their hydra heads, shouting the message of perpetuation of the race, more often than not, once again, to an unprepared mind. The immediate next set of thoughts that awaits its turn is the issue of providing for existence, both directly and indirectly.

These needs satisfied, the thoughts of assertion and manipulation re-assert themselves in the classic scenario of extending the influence of our thoughts, be it through power, money or brute physical strength that helps to establish the superiority in no uncertain terms. Manipulating situations and/ or people is a serious endeavor that requires essentials of perspicacity and pertinacious effort along with clear understanding of the influences on our thoughts. The reward of this effort is dominance, questioned or unquestioned over other competing minds.

The next logical step is to cocoon oneself in self-centered isolation that forms a barrier to the territorial infringement by thoughts at large, some of which may even be remotely related to the isolated thought under consideration. In this self-centered utopia, I come face-to-face with the ubiquitous question as to why the guilt perception is missing from the conscious perception in its formative essence. Answers are not only difficult to find but I am also left with an intriguing feeling.

The answers are lurking just on the periphery immediately beyond outlined boundaries that define the cognitive domain. These conflicts vie for recognition and are often mistaken for the boundaries of the confining thoughts.

The very purpose of these self-confining thoughts so generated, is to define artificial boundaries for the purpose of imposing unnatural confining limits on the scope, to enable us to deal with the thoughts in a manageable spectrum with a purpose to enhance the focus on the issue and permit manageability of the subject thought.

This is akin to dividing the food item in to bite sized pieces by the mother bird for easy ingestion by chicks in earlier example. This aims at food being eaten along with some other activity of perceived higher priority to us being performed simultaneously. Somewhat like popping edible bites in to the mouth and munching on it, as and when the possible breaks in the video game operation permit it.

Still later, even in the realm of self-actualization, the choice of the path to this goal is debated so fiercely, so as to put a fishmonger to shame. What we need to acknowledge, more than understand, is that there is a multiplicity when we look at the route to the goal of self-actualization but the aim of all the paths is the same.

Please note that I refrain from calling this as one, as the term one has an implied message of multiplicity; and term the goal as the divine singularity that is tentatively just beyond the reach. The very notion of something being tentatively beyond the reach essentially has a well-defined game-plan of encouraging people to strive hard and reach the goal breathing hard but with a breath to spare.

Please do permit me to indulge in purposeful simplification even at the risk of courting absurdity. Let us take an example of marketing. We do not wish or plan to force or even guide other people to reach a buying decision favorable to us by manipulating their thoughts.

The very fact guiding this seemingly virtuous course of action and thought is governed by the wake-up call, defining the end result as irreversible erosion of the brand equity.

If the target audience recognizes our effort to be, what it actually is, it is doomed to failure. The unstated message here is of simplification of this onerous task by rewriting the marketing and advertising rule book.

Our concerted effort should only be aimed at helping the potential customer for arriving at a decision which is essentially their own choice. This is a kind of scenario that is achieved only through developing alternatives and presenting these in such a manner that evaluation and selection criteria are firmly in place, before introduction of the viable alternatives.

It is in the domain of such predefined criteria that we may be permitted some operating leeway. This latitude is our sanctified space where we must perform our magic of swaying the audience opinion and influencing their thoughts to our benefit. *We do not sell; we only help people to reach a decision to buy from us.*

All this influencing and swaying must be done in such a manner so as to make the other people believe that they want to do, of their own volition, what we want them to do. This is leading us to the much maligned arena of manipulation. I find stigma associated with manipulation to be entirely incorrect and biased.

I believe that manipulation is the core theme of all marketing effort and management endeavor. To give an example, smell of freshly baked bread influences quite a few buying decisions, even when the target individuals are fully aware that there is no need for them to buy bread as this purchase will only add to the unused stock at home.

It is an established fact that, the sense of smell, unlike other sensory inputs, has an ability to bypass the logical thinking centers of the mind and can exert influence without being fully evaluated and hence, it is an important sensory input for the marketers to capitalize on with an aim of enabling buying decisions. However, there is a small issue involved here that, even this stratagem may be recognized by the target audience as a disguised attempt to force a buying decision.

The recognition of this influencing attempt may establish a negative bias that has a hidden risk of the seller being blacklisted by the buyer due to erosion of faith and may result in the compromise of brand value of seller, as perceived by the buyer.

Negative bias associated with manipulation has become very strong and well-entrenched in the fabric of operational methodology. The positive aspect of this wonderful tool has been completely forgotten and has been pushed to obscurity and direct application of this important tool has gone out of favor, although even the indirect usage is very powerful in its manifestation.

In the interest of reaping the rewards of this powerful tool, we have not only kept it alive but the unscrupulous practitioners have elevated status of this tool to the stature of an unofficial deity, who offers rewards at will, as and when asked for and at times largesse is bestowed even without the beneficiary having to ask for it. This is the kind of scenario that has elevated this tool of manipulation to such powerful status that we wish to unravel and understand it.

The need for understanding the mechanism of this phenomenon is further highlighted by wave upon wave of worshipers of this art form, who revel in the munificence of the handouts to the practitioners.

The best managers in the business have to be good manipulators of people by design. However, the blemish has taken such gargantuan proportions that, those who excel at this refined art form of interaction, tend to become closet practitioners swayed by the colossal mass of public and peer opinion.

These powerfully effective managers tend to start feeling guilty of their uncommon gift of positive people manipulation sooner than later. I have used the word positive here, to try and wash away the guilt association, though it remains to be seen, as to how much I have succeeded in my endeavor.

I shall at this time relate an example to showcase the powerful art of manipulation that results in unrestrained explosion of latent positive energy of such magnitude that even those, who are familiar with this phenomenon through prior experiences of the same, are left holding their breath, awestruck by the magnitude of unfolding events that find no parallel anywhere.

At one time, I was required to do some boring job of a report preparation that required endless tabulation without any great effort required of the brain. Since tackling the copious data and exercising endless permutations and combinations was quite taxing, I decided to exercise simple, direct manipulation.

It was a decision with some diffidence on my part as I was fully aware of the mundane nature of the work, which is why I did not want to do it myself.

I deliberately and quite mercilessly delegated the job to an unsuspecting colleague of mine, overemphasizing importance of the work and its visibility in the corporate framework. I also unashamedly indulged in highly praising the ability of the person to scale this insurmountable data mountain with a single minded purpose of the target person taking up the routine, boring work, with a feeling of gratitude towards me.

Then I very calmly took one oh – so – long coffee break. I do not really think that the person was taken in by my rhetoric, but to my utter surprise, the lady not only completed the job within the desired time frame and also produced the work of such great quality of the deliverable, which I could only hope to match in my dreams.

The work was done with spectacular effectiveness and superb quality. A lot of adjectives are used here. I have this serious deficiency of appreciating everything done well, especially if I cannot do the same myself. Actually this is not the last you are hearing of this as this theme will appear later also in this document.

I am saving the punch line for the grand finale as always. It is not only that I was rescued from doing a boring menial job, to cap it all, the lady, though harassed no end, also thanked me for having confidence in her abilities to entrust her with a job of such vital importance and visibility. This is the power of positive manipulation.

The very feeling that I have entrusted her with a job of serious importance, led to unleashing of the power of positive manipulation that not only the job was done well, in quick time and probably better than the quality of work I would have achieved, but I was also thanked for this unjust delegation.

However, I would like to caution a frivolous manipulator that it has taken me a lot of effort in direct teaching, supervising and mentoring to achieve the cult status that allows me such shameless manipulation opportunities today. There is a simple thought involved here.

I just take every day as a new one and take it upon myself to prove my worth to the group, ab initio, every single new day. We also have to be quick thinkers to keep people thinking positively of us, all the time.

There was a time, when I was accused of favoritism and partiality and justly so, as it turned out in the final analysis, establishing the fact for the chronicles.

I also should mention here that my culpability was only established in the postscript and then also in such a manner that I was not only found to be an eligible candidate for presidential pardon and was also adjudged to have been accused in a false and frivolous manner, with the accuser being reprimanded and being banished from the fraternity for all time.

It had so happened that as a motivational move, I had introduced a system, on weekly basis, of putting up names of top 5 performers on a notice board for all to see.

My logic was that those who find their names on the notice board will be elated and will keep pushing harder to remain there next week also and all others will strive harder to get their names on the honors list. However, it so happened that two names were stuck there with irritating (to some) regularity, hence the accusation.

Even the respected Rohit Agnihotri, was not spared and was asked by senior management to defend himself in an open forum. Not having any prior notice of unfolding events of such magnitude I was caught unawares.

It seems to me that what was not known to me at all was surely common knowledge as I could see some eager faces of people, belonging to other groups, who had come to witness the fall of the mighty.

When this grenade on a short fuse was lobbed in my unsuspecting lap, I had to think quickly, to be able to save my motivational move from being pushed to obscurity, as well as my reputation of being able to think on my feet and being one such person with whom no one wins an argument in the discussion arena.

Actually, it is quite difficult to get even a foothold to manage a bridgehead in the combat zones of the thought war that such a person may have brought upon himself.

I did get an idea in time and actually jumped up to state "I accept the accusation in all humility as the charge is an accurate one and I cannot and shall not try to escape responsibility. I only request to be allowed to own up my culpability without any interruption."

Now, when I had every one listening to me intently, all I said was "Yes, I accept that the charge is true and I am thankful to all of you for having brought this shortcoming in my operational repertoire to my notice; I am partial indeed, and have no qualms about it also." Before the sniggers could get too loud, I continued, "Yes, I am partial to good performance and actually am quite proud of this negative trait of mine." Applause broke out and I contentedly watched several faces inch closer to exits and then disappear quickly.

Major thought influences are:

•geography

•operational frame of reference

•peer pressure

•positive and negative vibes from other stakeholders

•influence of cult figures

•influence of extraneous thoughts

•influence of radical thoughts

•boredom

•fatigue

Suffice it to say that these above inputs are only a representative sample of the comprehensive set of such influences that can seriously affect our thoughts but the full detail is too large to be included here in this short commentary on this topic of serious importance.

The geography manifests itself through the influence of local customs, traditions and practices that are unique to the region whereas operational frame of reference has a much more inclusive effect on the thoughts, as it exerts an effect through the operating exigencies and work culture.

A simple example would be that the weekly off in Muslim countries is usually on Friday, the religious holy day of Muslim faith, as against Sunday in rest of the world.

When we finally have time to consider the world of young people, it will take us no time to realize that the most important influence on thoughts in this relatively vulnerable age group is peer pressure.

Peer pressure is the determinant factor, which drives young people to opt for uncommon hair arrangement and tattoos at this vulnerable age. This phenomenon is what, makes the older generation feel that, young people are getting out of hand and need to be rescued from the evils of body art, piercing of tongue & navel and torn clothes and a generally unkempt appearance. At the same time, the young people shout "generation gap" at the top of their voice to eschew all the offered words of advice as an unwarranted interference in their lives and cry foul to seek some personal space, which according to them is their birthright.

They avow that, they shall not permit any territorial infringement in their demarcated personal space. In this assertion young people seem to be all together and well-aligned. Influence of group vibes is also a strong part of the coercive environment that delivers the final out of shape, radical product.

Out of shape, in the view of oldies (uselessness implied); who do not have a life of their own and would not let the young people get one, if they can help it.

Then, there is the influence of cult figures. This time I shall not hide behind speech and appearance affectations but unequivocally state that the thoughts are highly influenced by cult figures like Abraham Lincoln, Albert Einstein, Elvis Presley, Amitabh Bachchan, Beatles, Chanakya, Erwin Rommel(the desert fox), John Fitzgerald Kennedy, Jennifer Lopez (J–LO), Karl Heinrich Marx, Madonna Ciccone, Mahatma Gandhi, Mao Zedong, Pandit Jawahar Lal Nehru, Paris Hilton, Sigmund Freud, S.G. Patton, Vladimir Ilyich Lenin and the greatest manipulator of the thoughts ever, **Adolf Hitler**.

His aim may have been questionable and even repugnant in the current context but his method was one of the most effective performances of all times that the world has witnessed.

We also must keep in perspective, all the time, the fact that history is written by winners and more often than not, it is a deliberate caricature of the defeated opponent that borders on the extreme and sometime, as in this case, gets in to ridiculous.

This is not to say that Hitler is to be worshiped but we may not make a caricature of the effective methodology and mode of rendering the message employed by now ridiculed and then (circa WWII), the most respected leader and highly influential figure of the Fatherland.

Next we have to deal with extraneous thoughts of the wandering mind. These normally would be of no use but sometimes these offshoots can engender radical thoughts that may lead us to the horizon of an entirely new beginning that was incomprehensible a short while ago.

These radical thoughts are many a time, labeled unreasonable along with the person who voices them, but these are the main sustaining force for radical changes, improvements and achievements.

Some people, propelled by their own nature or demands of the situation faced by us, have to take on the task of taking civilization to the next level of maturity, may find that they are labeled unreasonable by the very people they attempt to help and may have to carry this tag for a long undefined time before being redeemed by the now thankful world, which at this time acknowledges the value of their contribution and makes an effort to apologize for the ill-treatment meted out to them at an earlier time and to gratefully recognize the effort of these pioneers.

The unfortunate and unforgivable part is that for a large number of such talented people with great ideas, the recognition may be too late, many a time even after their demise.

This brings us to the inevitable unanswered question as to what is the use of appreciation that is accorded after end of existence of the individual being appreciated. Nothing!

This nothing creates a positive vacuum that tries to suck in everything around itself, not much unlike a black-hole, which sucks in everything in the vicinity and devours it all.

The black hole indeed is an entity that as per respected scientists will swallow all the mass of universe. When all the mass of the universe is assimilated in a single point of awesome gravity that holds all of the mass of the universe, it will be the defined time for the next Big Bang.

The pure energy, so released, once again will give birth to the mass that shall form the universe in a new edition.

The life of the departed individual has gone in vain. All the logic and reason that the person may have delved in during the unacknowledged lifetime has been a waste. I know that you want me to be reasonable.

We all make mistakes. At least the fact that we are willing to and actually do correct our mistake and confer the deserving honor posthumously should be appreciated and acknowledged.

The point that I wish to make here is that, we based on our delayed corrective action orientation, feel that we should be forgiven for our folly and should be treated fairly and in a just and reasonable manner that conforms to the social dictates of current time.

We must give it a thought whether we had treated the person, who has moved on, in a fair and reasonable manner and do we really deserve to be treated in a fair and reasonable manner, which would be antithesis of the idea in itself.

The query itself is so full of wrath, that sometimes we may choose the punishment for our wrongdoing instead of taking on the challenge of answering the question that shows us our ugly face in the crystal clear mirror of our own conscience, which may condemn us outright without waiting to hear the evidence that we wish to present in our defense.

The retribution meted out to us may be so harsh, so as to disallow any possible hope for reinstatement of our own being, in any discernible time frame, less than our own life time.

Last but not the least we have to deal with the issues of boredom and fatigue.

Boredom relates to the disinterest in whatever is being done, which may even be nothing at all. This nothing sometimes is the most difficult thing to decipher.

'It must be very difficult to do nothing. You may never know when you are done.'

The thought process is so influenced at this time by lethargy of inactivity that any thought of activity, which may have been rejected at other times, is very welcome now, as it represents the change of state that we yearn for.

At the other end of the spectrum, a fatigued mind may reject an activity that may have been welcome at any other time. It is to be understood that this denial is not absolute but has a temporal character and should be recognized as such and tested again later.

Let us now look at another set of thought influences in a different perspective:

•survival

•security

•comfort

•status

•Power (of manipulation)

Let us look at these aspects in a certain perspective that I hold in minor contempt, only because I do not have enough of it to hold it in utter contempt.

This is the perspective of money.

Let us take a look at what money means to us at various stages of life and various stages of maturity. Please note that I am choosing to make a clear distinction between aging and maturity and I am clearly stating that the two may not necessarily be the same.

The very first and most basic need money is called upon to serve is the survival, which also includes the need for ensuring perpetuation of the species in general and our own family line in particular.

Next, we move on to security which in modern times translates to steady income and a well-appointed home instead of the brawn and weapons of the earlier times, which were the needed attributes of the time to earn food and keep it safe from competitors.

The very next items trying to seek our attention are comfort needs like air-conditioning and soft beds along with a well- appointed kitchen, well-equipped rest rooms and a BMW in the garage. Next item is the status. Quite frequently and it is almost by design that there is a considerable overlap in the comfort and status zones.

The most sought after quality and also the most satisfying ability that money confers upon us is the power to control other minds and thereby exercise control over the bodies associated with these minds controlled by the money power in our hands.

There is also a related topic of setting the target (aim) that is intrinsic to the ongoing discussion, but I choose to include just the following quote that says a lot, once we start thinking about it.

"The greater danger, for most of us is not that our aim is too high and we miss it, but that it is too low and we reach it." - *Michelangelo*

The wisdom represented here is a valuable asset to the human conscience and should be so respected and preserved. Conscience is a flag that gets raised when we are operating too close to the boundaries defined by generally accepted societal norms and when there is a recognizable probability that we may transcend it. The two reasons for low targets are low self-esteem (low self-confidence) and/ or simple unadulterated laziness. The society that allows individuals to get away with setting low targets is equally responsible for this regressive attitude that allows people to get away with non-performance as much as the lazy person.

We shall limit ourselves to simple thoughts to begin with, before we take on the challenge of trying to understand complex thoughts. To achieve happiness seems to be a simple enough thought to me that within itself carries a goal, an aim to accomplish and a target to attain.

Though we have a clear-cut scenario, when we get to thinking about it, we tend not to think of the goal as being happy; because although this goal is unambiguous, happiness itself does not lend to any unique definition, as it is person dependent; actually dependent on the current perception of the person. Even this can be rationalized a bit, if we are able to agree upon a common minimum set of goals. Then it is certain that the person-dependent variance can be managed to a reasonable extent to serve our purpose at this time. Happiness for me may just be lazing around and being what now-a-days is termed as being couch or mouse potato; while you energetic fellows may term it sheer lethargy and actually may wonder as to how someone can term it happiness.

Happiness for you young fellows would probably be the immediate aftermath of your morning five mile run that leaves you with an internal glowing and sometimes also a gloating feeling, which you find to be sheer delight.

So we, more often than not, are likely to use alternative expressions that have better form and offer better understanding potential and most important of all, higher person to person portability for the term, so defined. This helps in defining and acceptance of the happiness goal in a generic format.

We generally seem to be using the term success as a substitute for happiness even though it does not translate with good enough fidelity.

The reason being that right or wrong, fit or misfit; we do have some measures for success, whereas happiness does not seem to fit that easily in to any defined format, design or structure.

So we tend to look for and try to find some numerical equivalents that lend themselves easily for the purpose of comparisons, which guide our derived perceptions and influence our thoughts.

These quantitative assessments may not be the true representation of the measure but are generally accepted as valid content, due to the lack of a better option.

We tend to measure success numerically but it would be a folly to base our assessment entirely on the quantitative measure.

It is, at this time that we do not wish to entirely depend upon the objective numerical assessment, which we usually respect highly and include qualitative assessment, needed by the demand of the time, even at the risk of whole gamut of analysis becoming subjective and consequently non-reproducible.

We shall see and recognize this as an acceptable deviation. I do have a saying for this also:

'Do not be obsessed with success; try to be competent and capable; success will follow automatically'

Here again, I have a word of caution; this automatic success may not fit any preconceived notion of a definite pattern or design.

This is a must caution device, in absence of which, the brand success may be relegated to obscurity, because we have committed the most atrocious crime of our age of not having proper anticipated labels at expected location on its face. I choose to introduce three terms at this stage that shall have important bearing on the discussion that shall be introduced later. These are:

Consciousness

Super-consciousness

Supreme consciousness

Consciousness by its intrinsic nature of individual orientation has certain definite restrictions, whereas super-consciousness has the advantage of being able to acquire additional inputs through extra sensory perception, which is beyond cognizance for the person-centric awareness.

This requires us to act confidently in cognizable space with an assurance of being on the right track, which will take us to the defined goal. This confidence is the key to success of our endeavor.

From this level we graduate to looking at supreme consciousness, which is the all-enveloping super set of cognizance. This supreme consciousness, in many of its expressions is entirely beyond sensory perception, though it permits a brief look to those who strive for this glimpse with correctly focused orientation and good intentions.

The ways to the super consciousness are all through submission and require assimilation of the individual entity in the larger group entity, with derived views of acquired attributes, use of which, for deciphering the purpose of our being, is the key to hallowed portals where we are not permitted an entry, as yet.

So, we take this opportunity to prove that we are worthy inheritors and deserve access to the knowledge portal, as the recognized members of the group of deserving souls.

It is the manifested trait of detachment that allows the supreme entity, an ability to have an overall view while all the time being in touch with the obvious.

It is to some extent like watching a game where none of our favorite teams are playing. This detachment gives us an ability to concentrate on the intrinsic quality of the game and ponder upon the outcome as an unattached observer.

This is exactly the manner, in which the Hindu philosophy of life teaches us to perform when we, ourselves, are the actors. This, however, as would be expected, is not all that easy and we must be able to exercise a lot of control over sensory perceptions, to be able to live through life in this manner.

The assimilation of our being in to the supreme consciousness is our ultimate aim and we have to follow the path of complete dedication and unreserved submission. However, we have another orientation in this space and we shall touch upon both the paths to enable selection of one of these, if required.

These two ways are: Gyan and Bhakti; the knowledge and worship routes. Worship route is virtuous and only requires complete submission and is considered to be easy and is recommended for general practitioners.

On the other hand, knowledge route is highly challenging, infinitely more demanding, extremely difficult to practice and is suggested only for those individuals who are free from bonds of responsibility towards the society and immediate family and are judged to be above the common lot in terms of acquired knowledge and wisdom and considered to be endowed with the highest degree of intelligence and discerning ability.

Wait a minute. There is one more path called the 'Hatha yoga'. This path is definitely not for the general practitioners.

This approach has certain overtones of achieving and/ or acquiring the article of desire almost by force and this conceited approach, may not be acceptable to all.

This essentially is a demand, for something that in our considered opinion, we not only deserve but also feel that allocation of just reward is overdue. This also communicates that we consider ourselves to be eligible.

Worship route is easy and there are rewards also, in terms of increased ability to handle tension and worries, which have become integral part of our work and home life nowadays. The other cognizable benefit comes from the overall view that we get access to, which helps us to acknowledge and understand the importance of the routine work, which we may have thought to be mundane.

This discussion leads us to a seriously controversial topic that I expected and planned to take up later in this book.

There is this one concept, in Hindu philosophy, which western way of thinking finds hard to get a grip on. This elusive concept, which the western group of thinkers, representing a body of knowledge that finds it difficult to question itself, based on the logic that belief is beyond inquiry; tend to reject and to a lesser degree deride.

The most knowledgeable are those; who know that they know not.

Re-incarnation:

Now we try to address this difficult concept that many a time has daunted a lot of thinkers across geographies, age groups, cultures, generations and the constituents of the most evolved civilizations that time has witnessed.

Let us try to see as to why this impossible has remained impossible across ages and beyond cognition to all those, who have, in a suicidal moment, got ensnared into this ever inviting spider web of unnerving and mesmerizing cataclysm. The essence of the concept is accessible only through methods that are beyond sensory perception.

The problem here is that western way of life and thinking brutally inculcates a trait in people that permits cognition of only those entities and ideas that are accessible through sensory perceptions.

This imposed boundary limits the horizon and excludes extrasensory perception to the detriment of practitioners. This, in itself, is such a statement that I almost expect someone to dutifully challenge it, as if I have brought this upon myself by design. Long before I hear a snicker, I wish to clarify that I am not talking about a sleight of hand magic here but an all-enveloping illusion that has the power to manifest itself, if it chooses to do so.

I am not even referring to the all-powerful God at this time, as minor things like this discussion and associated chaos I can easily handle myself. I shall indeed invoke God when I really need help. I guess that you may not believe me as this assertion does sound a bit arrogant, even to me.

Okay, if you do not believe me read on. Oh yes, please do read on, even if you believe me, dear paying customers. Actually it is your belief in me that imbues the confidence in me, to be so assertive about the thought coming up now. This is my show stopper dear patrons; so please put down the bag of chips in your lap and free your hands to deliver the applause that my hypothesis deserves.

The goal of logical inquiry, which is quest for elusive, is to arrive at a complete set of questions that are germane to the discussion and relevant to the pursuit. I now present my piece de resistance, wrapped in a question that enhances the flavor of the offering.

Why do we need to look for physical manifestation of everything? Many a time, a thought in itself is a complete main course and does not need to redeem itself with a physical expression that we can sense, feel and touch.

Let us then free the re-incarnation of its physical bondage of re-birth as is generally accepted but actually is merely a common, garden variety misconception in my considered opinion, for all that it is worth.

Lot of talk; then what exactly is this re-incarnation? I do think, and also agree with the learned audience, that this appetizer has been interesting but let us not put the customers off.

This prelude is sufficient enough to whet the appetite of the audience with high expectations.

Here is the main entree:

Let us think of re-incarnation as continuation of the acquired knowledge assimilated into wisdom within an endless continuum that has neither a defined beginning nor a definite end but may extend ad-infinitum, beyond the cognizable domain.

We are essentially talking about the continual evolution of thought, irrespective of the survival of the human body in which the thought resides temporarily for a short period, that is, but a fleeting moment in the context of cosmic awareness and almost infinite time lines. I do believe that some more detail may be useful here for the uninitiated minds that may exist even among the representative body of my learned audience.

I think that this concept is best explained in the dimension of the Guru (teacher) and Shishya (disciple) Parampara (tradition) of learning that was prevalent in the ancient Hindu civilization, which dates before any other, in terms of maturity, awareness and wisdom.

We are indeed talking not of mere intelligence but of great body of evolved wisdom represented by the greatest and most accomplished thinkers on the face of earth, both in temporal and spatial dimensions. The method and medium of learning was oral instruction and the learning was a direct influence to the cultivation of mind, thereby contributing to the body of knowledge without any latency for being analyzed and assimilated in to wisdom. This scheme also precludes any possibility of incomplete or inaccurate understanding of the information being communicated as the knowledge being bestowed is understood concurrently and in a synchronous manner.

The greatness derives from the fact that these great minds with no parallel anywhere, were also the most humble and this humbleness permitted them to accept that they are but a microcosm in the physical body, both in age and strength compared to the infinite universe.

This realization also enabled them to acknowledge that the grasp of their highly evolved minds, though gigantic by any existing standards, then or now, was yet a miniscule entity in comparison to the smallest atom of the supreme consciousness.

This realization allowed these extraordinary minds to understand and acknowledge that even with the fully dedicated application of the greatest minds of all time, only such a small part of the target objective could be achieved, so as to be negligible.

This realization necessitated that evolution of thought towards the target objective should be continued through several generations. The World Wide Web, collaborative work tools, huge data and information repositories are all manifested extensions of this realization by the human race that all its constituent individuals are subject to the finality of death.

Today, in this age the biggest surprise is that everyone is knowledgeable about the reality and finality of death but only very few are prepared for it or plan for the event. In fact, it is very common to come across people, who harbor an untenable thought that they will be able to defy death by seeking even the most ridiculous and almost pathetic measures and methods to be immortal.

The ancients not only realized and understood it but also planned for it by developing the concept of re-incarnation, which essentially is a method to carry forward, acquired knowledge and evolved wisdom trapped in a dying body.

This is accomplished by transmitting this wealth of knowledge and wisdom to the young minds supported by young healthy bodies. It may yet take a lot of time for the young minds endowed with this wealth to take cognizance of their inheritance, which is a highly evolved knowledge set that may be beyond their comprehension, at this time.

In due course of time, using the tools imparted by the Guru, these disciples will start to work on the inheritance and take evolution of the thought further, before transferring the tools and annotated wisdom of the ages to the next set of inheritors to take this effort forward in similar cycles, till the targeted objective is attained.

Development of the thought, its analysis and/ or assimilation continues without any interruption after its transfer from teacher to disciple.

This continual development of the thought is enabled as transfer of thought is along with the essential tools to facilitate further development of the thought, which is assigned responsibility of the inheritors.

Actually, this process gets strengthened as the idea under development and its associated assemblage are being worked upon by the tools of same nature and properties over a great period of time, as required, to effectively contribute to the inheritance.

So, the method and tools remain same and number of like-minded practitioners increases many-fold. The ideas so developed, in this well-planned implementation methodology, get enriched by additional inputs of the mind, in which they reside for yet another short period of time.

This sequence, in which the idea traverses multiple minds over a long period of time that represents the existence of several generations, also contributes to the continuous testing of the idea against new parameters and yardsticks, as they are presented by the dynamically changing environment and also evolving circumstances of the relevant time-frame.

This process helps to streamline the thought by removing the accumulated debris over a number of iterations. This is needed to ensure that alignment of the thought to the current perspective is maintained.

This also contributes to the refining and further enriching of the subject thought that has traversed a number of minds, representing several generations, before being considered for inclusion in the wisdom repository, which is the ultimate aim of our tenacious effort.

Though, admittedly, effort gets distributed but focus remains aligned as the method and tools being used are the same and only additional work items are the monitoring for alignment through planned interactions and integration of these work products in the format of targeted deliverable.

The hardliners will jump up to be recognized and would offer hard evidence to the dogs of cynicism in the form of young people who remember the details of their past lives. Still another set will claim that re-incarnation is the cornerstone of the Hindu Dharma (religion) and make an assertion that I am indulging in sacrilege by inventing an alternative interpretation.

This scenario is fraught with problems that I fully understand and I know that I must face this opprobrium as all radical thinkers have to face this disgrace and like all other people before me I must take on this ignominy and dishonor outcome as inevitable.

At this time I wish to re-introduce the important topic of desire. What is desire and how does it manifest itself? Desire is a deeply and strongly felt emotion.

Desire is such a strong emotion that I believe, it should be accorded its due in terms of the central positioning in the expressed thought spectrum as uncrowned king of the realm.

First of all, we tend to think of the desired entity. I hesitate to use the term object of desire only due to my choice of example (desire personification) to be used to explain this thought.

We make an attempt to get close to the desired entity. The next level of thought accentuation is to make an effort to acquire or access the same in a manner commensurate with strength of our feeling of desire for the target entity.

Next element, representing consequential emotion is the fear that caters for even the near negligible possibility of our attempt being unsuccessful.

Then, if we are actually unsuccessful in our attempt, this gives rise to anger which is proportional to the perceived strength of the stronghold of this emotion on our resultant thoughts related to achievement or non- achievement of the objective.

Anger is another all-encompassing strong emotion that robs us of the capability of rational thought. Now, a person having lost the ability of rational thought gets almost hypnotized by the events taking place and the emotional thoughts that are representation of our hurt feelings, which are exceptionally powerful negative influence.

In this state of mind, a person does not possess the ability to think coherently and act in a rational manner and at this stage chooses to accept the inevitable. When this catastrophe takes hold of us, it is as bad as having lost our conscience, which has the potential of eradicating our very existence as an assured outcome of our proclivity for irrational thought and action.

This is an important manifestation and must be kept in the perspective to avoid transgression of societal norms. Now, I go to the promised example. In a crowded party I notice a beautiful girl at the edge of the assemblage and gravitate towards her in an inhibited and defensive manner. I control my urge of running away due to lurking fear of rejection and finally manage to ask her for the next dance.

She gives me an encouraging smile that further captivates me but refuses to accept. The engaging smile that I was accorded had put my hopes up and hence the rejection hurt much more.

I turn away in anger, which is further compounded when I see her moving towards the dance floor hand in hand with another person, who in my opinion definitely did not deserve the honor. Now, I get really mad and devoid of all rational thought; bash up this intruder as if by eliminating the irritating presence I will get to step in the now vacant slot.

Of course, this does not happen and I actually get greatly humiliated and get thrown out of the party and now I am feeling lower than the lowest life form and have been completely obliterated from the cognizance spectrum of the desired entity and my desperate hope has no future.

I feel like death and it actually is that, in terms of visual perception of the thought-scape of person concerned and I do not have any hope of realizing my dream. I counter the excoriation I am being subjected to, only halfheartedly. How is it to be concluded that I am saying what these individuals think I have said?

I choose not to engage these people at this time. I actually do not care if my strategic retreat is termed desertion. Actually being called a deserter by a certain set of people is an honor and these people will understand my insinuation and its implication in no uncertain terms. I only hope and pray to God that this understanding helps them to become better human beings.

What I am experiencing at this moment is result of choices and decisions made in the past, sometimes very recent past; what I will experience in future depends on choices and decisions I make now.

Happiness is a daily decision.

Each morning, when we wake up, we face the inevitable moment when we have to decide whether it is going to be a good day or a bad day.

Some of us make a choice of a good day and then take it upon ourselves to make it a great day. Another set of people choose to call it a murky bad day and decide to indulge in self-pity that becomes their comfortable cocoon and they settle down to embrace inaction and this choice of inaction further accentuates the downside of the day that has already been labeled a bad day.

This whirlpool does not allow such people to escape and sucks them in. Many people of this set recognize the folly of their choice and try to induct corrective action. The fact that they may not succeed is irrelevant.

The important thought is that these people have tried to make a difference. It is too late and nothing can save them from the whirlpool of mediocrity that inaction brings in its wake. This curse sneaks upon people with such stealth so as to put to shame the strategic stealth bomber of the caliber of Northrop Grumman B-2 Spirit. Then there are yet another set of people, who do not fit the spectrum and always aim at something beyond the offered choices.

This set of people are likely to choose the great day option which is not a currently available option but an aim achievable with highly focused effort, a type of stretch target that requires extending oneself to the limit to be actualized.

Our life is all about choices and informed selection of the course of action from available choices. Let us not forget those who make their own rules and work hard to create an option favored by them which did not appear in the offered list of options at the outset. Please take a note that this additional option created by the people of exceptional ability and positive attitude towards life is not available for the benefit of all, though it should be.

· *You choose how to react to situations*

· *You choose how other people affect your mood*

· *You choose how you will live your life*

Last but not the least; someone can insult you only because you have permitted and enabled them to do so.

A good idea is never to let anyone know that they have the power to hurt you.

Rohit Agnihotri

ESSENCE

'We need air, water and food to be alive, but we come alive with sex.'

Speech is the oral expression of our thoughts whereas our actions are the physical manifestation of our thinking in general and our specific thoughts in particular.

Sometimes we launch into action without a fully developed thought pattern and tend to fill in the gaps as we move along the road less traveled, and then, as would be expected, end up being caught unawares, at times.

We need to guard against this impulse of launching into action with thoughts that are as yet underdeveloped and may need the time they deserve, to ripen and reach fruition. Thoughts are powerful tools.

It would be an utter folly to disregard the power of thought in standalone and/ or related context. Thought is the time honored dimension of reality that deals with perception in its physical manifestation.

"Nothing is more powerful than an idea, whose time has come." **- Victor Hugo**

This must not be trifled with, as it conjugates with nature's fury that brings on unbridled devastation and at the same time also the constructive power of genesis that heralds the arrival of a new beginning that has the promise of great bounty and thereby welfare of all.

The following simple statement aims to put the essence of the power of thoughts in correct perspective.

"Whether you think you can, or you think you cannot -- you are right" *- Henry Ford*

73

The refined thought behind this simple statement is that there is no such thing as reality.

Reality and perception:

Everything in this universe or at least the cognizable part of it is all perception. This is definitely an ambitious statement. I do realize and recognize that it may not be easy for all of us to accept and agree with this assertion.

There is no reality, all reality is only perception

The important issue about simple things is that overt bias of simplicity makes it eminently acceptable and also highly difficult to refute or even argue with. This is indeed a radical thought which is aimed to change our perception of reality; which, as per earlier assertion is reality itself.

Temporal aspect, to which every reality is beholden haplessly, comes to our rescue to irrevocably establish the perception orientation of all reality. Every individual perceives the reality only as what they can relate to. What I cannot feel or sense the presence of, cannot be reality.

Let me try to make this concept easier to understand by introducing another less complicated thought. I shall now talk of actual reality and perceived reality. I intend to tackle the borderline difference between the two stated entities. If the fact be known, this entire last sentence is not for audience consumption. I am challenging myself to think hard and get me out of this quandary, where I have landed myself. I do need something substantive to deliver myself from the sharp horns of dilemma where I have somehow managed to ensconce myself with great ability and no forethought. I must find a way out of this predicament to be able to define perception of reality and the reality itself.

If you read the last paragraph again, something I have had to do a few times, it is easy to see that I am talking about myself as if I am two different people merged in to one. This perceived duality and the attempt to escape from this perplexing spider web of the quandary, I am faced with, which is holding me captive, is the core concept of hypothesis I am about to put forward. We must take time and make the necessary effort to set ground rules so that the discussion does not get disparate and lose its sanctity. What is this perception orientation which is being touted so much here?

Perception is the foretaste of reality. Which reality are we talking about now? Actual reality or yet another perception, since we have already stated that all reality is only perception. Now, we need to talk about perceived reality that includes its environment as the necessary attachment, else it becomes lost in the quagmire of orphaned ideas, which are actually aborted thoughts.

Some of our friends may think that this is getting too complex and probably is of no value and I cannot use this line of thinking to arrive at a substantive doctrine or even do something meaningful with this line of thought. Where is all this leading us? What else but another quotation.

"If we all did the things we are capable of doing, we would literally astound ourselves."
- Thomas Edison

The feeling of helplessness is anyway not going to get us anywhere. Please do keep a positive attitude as it will lead us to something useful and may even deliver us from routine drudgery of every consecutive day and lead us to pursue a worthy endeavor, enriching our lives.

I am also asked some very basic questions sometimes, which irritate me no end. So, I have prepared stock answers for the typical presumptuous questions like:

What is your outlook on life?

The stock answer that I deliver with a smile is:

My blood group and my attitude towards life is the same

B+

"Positive attitude may not solve all your problems, but it will annoy enough people to make it worth the effort." - Herm Albright

We need to talk about perception of reality in the context, which all of us can easily relate to. We shall talk about thirst.

Let us first take up the fact that feeling thirsty is only a perception and not reality. We must keep in perspective the temporal and spatial aspects to be able to better understand this narrative and arrive at an understanding.

When I say that I am feeling thirsty, it is very easy to comprehend that I am referring to a perception.

Now let us look at the temporal aspect. If we continue to ignore this feeling or perception of thirst, we shall, in due course of time, reach a state of dehydration, which can only be addressed by imbibing suitable quantity of water to address and alter the thirst perception. The point here is that, the reality is not really absent or even dissociated; it is only at a different location in the temporal space.

All that is happening here is that, most often we deal with the perception (of thirst) and alleviate the possibility of coming face to face with the reality, which in this perspective is the state of dehydration.

The point I am making is that, the perceptions are so powerful that we deal with the perceptions and do not get to the touch modality of interaction with reality. What I cannot touch or feel cannot be real. Since, the actual event, please allow me to call it reality for a few moments in this context, is beyond my cognitive domain at this time, hence for me it does not exist at all.

What is not cognizable for me does not exist in my version of the universe defined by the cognitive boundaries of my awareness which is limited by the reach of my ability to think as an individual.

The purpose of life, actually our being; is to continually keep working on expanding these cognitive boundaries with the ultimate aim of this exercise targeted at cosmic awareness that may give us a fleeting glance of eternity at the singularity, we talked about earlier.

It may be as difficult for you, as it is for me, to understand this concept of the fleeting glance of eternity. Actually, it is quite simple. It indeed is a fleeting glance that is frozen in time to allow us a larger window of time to come to grips with the information item, or shall I say visual snapshot that allows us to study it in relative luxury of time that is otherwise not accorded to us.

This phenomenon is akin to my snatching a moment from the fast moving blips of time that incessantly keep moving future to present and present to past relentlessly in the time perspective, which is a framework we can relate to.

Now we come across another problem of preserving the character of the frozen time slice that we have snatched from the unceasing march of time.

The problem here is that, we have incarcerated a moment in time, but one, who is imprisoned, cannot be happy; one, who is in captivity, cannot laugh and cannot come alive

This is what I alluded to when I mentioned about preserving the character of the time slice. The second item in this context is about the spatial reference.

We are still with the example of thirst. One scenario is that I am sitting at home a few meters from the refrigerator that holds refreshing cold bottles of finest potable water on the planet and/ or ice cold beer cans.

My perception of thirst gets influenced by the near availability of the needed item. So I do not feel as thirsty as I actually am, because I know that at any time of my choice, I can slake my thirst by reaching for the object of desire in quick time and with little effort.

So, I worry about losing the thread of thought instead and continue writing this text for some more time and am able to defer the thirst need without any anxiety.

Here, I actually am, so much more worried about losing continuity of thought that the perception of thirst gets diluted without any conscious effort on my part.

Now we take up the second scenario of being stranded in the middle of the Thar Desert situated in the western part of Indian sub-continent, miles away from any trace of civilization.

Now when I get thirsty, because of the knowledge that water is not available anywhere near, the thirst becomes acute in a very short time and demands to be addressed on a priority higher than any other.

The purpose of this example is to demonstrate for recognition, the influence of associated information elements and also the knowledge whirlpools, on the thought being currently experienced or contemplated on another plane of consciousness.

The thought spectrum is a seriously cluttered place with all kind and types of thoughts, feelings, Impressions, and experiences competing for recognition and being assigned biased priorities that they wish to quarrel with but find themselves muzzled by the demands of establishing currency (applicability in the present domain) and can do nothing but bide their time, hoping for an opportune time to demand their due of the limelight.

Innermost core of the consciousness is the altar, where Genesis, Evolution, Maturity, and Oblivion phases are faced by the thoughts. Let us further dissect it to analyze the makeup of the inner core.

This seems to consist of, intelligence, conscience, ego, pride and conceit at the first look.

Now that we have painstakingly established the basic tenets of the thought array, we can tackle some important questions such as:

What is knowledge? What can we know? And the most important question of them all, what is worth knowing? Who can tell?

Not me surely. Those who know do not assertively declare the fact of their knowledge and those who offer to lecture on the issue, definitely do not know.

Humility comes intrinsically bundled with knowledge and it is this humbleness, strategically imbued, which prevents the knowledgeable to proclaim their knowledge from the rooftops.

Actually when we look at this from another angle it may not sound so humble after all. One, who knows, also knows intuitively that, what and how much is not known. This perspective instinctively tells us that, what we even think that we know, is an infinitesimal part of 'what can be known' set of knowledge.

This realization of insignificance of our knowledge with respect to the colossal body of 'what can be known' set of knowledge, effectively prevents us from making any tall claims of access and/ or retention of the point of reference of knowledge, in the targeted cognitive segment.

This recognition leads us to the realization, in an anticipated manner and as an expected outcome that the microscopic bit part that we may have achieved cognition of, is so minute, that it does not deserve any affirmative achievement recognition at all.

So the outcome of the analysis is that, if I say I know all that can be known, I am a fool and even if I admit that I do not know what can be known and definitely not the distinction of what can be known and what is worth knowing, it is just a fact. There is no element of humility in this space. If it is termed being humble by me or anyone else, all that is needed to be said is that, if one is being humble, then there indeed is, a lot to be humble about.

Make no mistake, I am indeed indulging in severe criticism that borders on abrasive excoriation for one, who thinks that there is even an iota of known, in individual capacity, within the 'what can be known' segment.

So we employ the face saving device of addressing 'what is worth knowing' and land our unsuspecting toes in still more hot water than where we were, to begin with, for this question is far more complex and still more difficult to answer, than the question we tried to escape from.

Since I do not have an answer for this, let me attempt to try to address the question by elaborating upon it, in a hope that somewhere along the line, we might get a suitable pointer that may take us close to the targeted ultimate answer.

First of all, we need to establish a comprehensive set of questions. Then we run through these questions to establish, as to which all of these questions can be answered and then only we may reach the premise where we can talk about 'what is worth knowing'.

You may have noticed that when I tried to slip a fast one by changing the question I got snared in to the trap of necessarily answering the question of 'what can be known' before I even attempt the question of as to 'what is worth knowing'.

Actually, even before this, I need to address the question of 'what is knowledge'. As always, I shall take the easy option and say that the collected facts organized as information and represented in the rational relational pattern is knowledge. Now we can include analytical expression to arrive at coherent inferences that guide us to employ replication in high occurrence scenarios.

This is evolution of related set of inferences in to what is commonly referred to as the wisdom.

As an individual, I do not have any quarrel with those who do not know and know that they do not know and are also willing to admit this highly prevalent inadequacy.

I do have a problem, to put it mildly, with those of us, who do not know and also know not that they do not know. This group can be written off as this attitude precludes any possibility of strategic learning even at a later stage.

Now we try to address 'what is worth knowing'. Please note that I am only saying that we address the question and make no mistake, I am definitely not trying to answer this complex question. It is far too complicated for my limited abilities and I have no reservations about admitting it, for I wish to remain in the group of those who know that they know not, and at this juncture have no plan to slip in to the classification of the written off bunch.

In the ocean of silence you may discover your eternal treasures of peace, love and happiness. In silence, you can let bad feelings and past sorrows dissolve. In the ephemeral silence, you can hear the whisper of God saying, "Come, my child and rest with me. You are a peaceful soul."

With the blessings of God almighty, I now build up courage to express my views on another much debated topic that intrigues all living beings that come to be touched upon by this powerful emotion called **'love'**. This is another very strong emotion that demands center stage positioning above all others and forces unconditioned devotion and unreserved acceptance.

The feeling of love is a great one. It just has to touch people to inculcate the feeling of well- being in them and instantly change them for the better.

We come in contact with someone, we come to know them closely, then we tend to care for them, then we know them still better and fall in love with them. I hate this term of falling in love. In my opinion for all it is worth, we actually rise in love and allow ourselves to profess all that is humane and lovable about ourselves and then get on with the act of permeating this feeling of love all across the spectrum we are part of, in a single minded approach that overcomes all obstacles in its path, in a powerful manner.

There is fraternal love, love for our progeny, love for our family, love for our society, love for our nation and finally love for human race and ultimately for all living beings including plant life and even single cellular organisms, with whom we cohabit the planet earth.

The way it is described here, love seems to be a well thought out process outcome rather than a spontaneous occurrence that we normally associate with the feeling of love. What about love at first sight?

We take a first look at our newborn and we immediately rise in love with the infant, do we not? Actually it is a long drawn conditioning process, where we are aware of the upcoming event and are mentally prepared to love our offspring at the first sight. For the mother, this process is much more intimate as the growth of the embryo within her own body is a continual reminder and the perpetual conditioning for the birth event, which is a much awaited happening with another set of associated thoughts.

Please note that I have managed to veer the discussion to safe ground, where I have very certain terrain and am sure of finding approval of the audience. Wait a minute; I am not ducking the question you have in mind. I know this question that you have been waiting to ask ever since I started on this strain of the discussion, namely, love at first sight with a person of opposite sex.

Now my entire facade is laid bare, for I cannot hide behind theory of preconditioning anymore; a theory that saved my unmentionable in the discourse on the last topic just before this. Please do not forget that I am an onion type of person and may have several facade layers before, if at all, the inner core is laid bare, which again may be made up of still more layers.

Now I choose to define this instant cup of noodles variety of love using the laws of attraction. Men are attracted to women who display the numeric measure characteristics of a good child bearing chalice.

Women always look for men, who in their perception can provide for good upbringing of the offspring. The upbringing aims at security, which in current times has taken on an unmistakable financial hue, but best part of the good upbringing ability relates to social status and the respect commanded by the person among peers.

At another plane of thought, people also tend to be attracted to those individuals who do not seem to be noticing them at all. This is the domain of challenges. We love to accept and overcome challenges as this is a definite ego boost for us. In the real world, out of these pages, this is referred to as playing hard to get. This stratagem often yields the desired outcome.

We also tend be attracted to people who praise us, another ego boosting phenomenon. If the challenge is too daunting, this may put us off. So the technique employed is to remain out of grasp, but within reach, a stretch target to be realized with extraordinary effort.

Next item in this list is the main marketing plank for all the beauty related article sellers of the world and the mainstay of the selling ploys employed by the cosmetics and perfume sellers of the world.

This is what is used by the beautiful gender of the species to further embellish their visage with the purpose of attracting the opposite gender specimen, aimed at the sole purpose of perpetuating the race.

Even the good looking and nice smelling fruit is a simple ploy to attract the medium for dispersal of seed, such as humans, birds or other animals with a single point agenda of preserving the race by continuation in next generation of plants through earlier mentioned wide dissemination of the seed to extend the reach of the race and support evolution. Next item is an often quoted 'opposites attract'. This is based mainly on our trait of curiosity, which in one story killed the cat but helps here in continuation of the race. However this expression is entirely true in one specific orientation.

Opposite genders attract. No doubt about it and this happens long before the member of the species is fully equipped with ability to procreate. The basic need for reproduction is deeply ingrained in our genes and takes hold of our thoughts, emotions and actions even before we are fully aware of the repercussions or awake to the consequences as the outcome.

Next item dictates that we keep some secrets; this again feeds the ego, for when the secrets are revealed one at a time, there is a regular feed for the ego demon that demands its due and with all the secrets revealed may tend to move on to fresh challenges and new mysteries.

Here, the social structure is likely to be compromised and so we lean on the filial attachments and connubial love bonds. The conjugal demands, needs and rights exercise their due and keep the family and society together in the face of strong challenges that use these same basic lures as their tool and threaten to collapse the carefully built social structure that abides by the preset norms and the force of still more basic enticements of race perpetuation.

Adolf Hitler took it too far, but call of this basic need of providing for suitable upbringing environment for young of the race by eliminating competition may be an effective method aligned with doctrine of "survival of the fittest', though the means employed were surely abhorrent.

Next emotional thought that we take up is romance. Please note that romance is not exclusively related to feelings of affection of a certain kind.

This is just a niche expression of romance that has mostly been limited to the affection domain. Though, I do not claim that this is not it, but I wish to state that this is only a single facet of the expression of romance.

Romance in its full frame expression is primarily about achieving what seems to be unattainable or simply beyond reach in first cut analysis and expressed orientation of the immediate nature. Some thoughts are serial in nature while the other set is parallel. To give an example of the serial and parallel thoughts, we look in to hunger.

Origin of hunger is the bodily need for nourishment, which needs to be satisfied with food intake. The food intake satisfies the primary physical need of nourishment.

Since we were feeling hungry, the mind directs body to eat a little extra so that a similar need should not reoccur too soon. When we eat extra food, this leads to physical sluggishness.

Lethargy takes hold of our thoughts and we indulge in siesta. Next, we wake up well rested, relaxed in body and mind, feeling quite energetic to take on the world at our own terms.

Now the other perspective should get the deserved focus. In the same example above; no, I am not running out of the examples; using the same example is to serve the purpose of keeping the context in perspective and also to enable comparison in similar environment with an objective of putting to rest, the bias accusation even before it is voiced.

Picking up the thread of conversation once again, we consider a scenario where we have available, the multiple food options that vie for our attention, with each food item engaging us in a thought journey of flavor voyage, which is the Shangri-La incarnate for discerning palate of the connoisseurs, who lend their epicurean taste buds to a consortium of flavor textures from across the geographical spread.

The offered victual delights, boasting of a lineage spanning across generations of inventive effort, vie for favor, in this journey of gastronomical delectation; for appreciation of aficionados of the culinary art; which is the noblest, purest and most ardent love, ever experienced.

Now, the thoughts experienced about the taste of each of these edible offerings compete for favor all at one time and need to be observed in a parallel manner, as no one thought is willing to wait, while others go ahead.

Although this may not exactly be a scenario of first come first served, but we all know value of the first impression. This thought multitasking is all fine but in an obvious difference, thought multitasking and action multitasking bring out the contentious nature of multitasking that forces a decision to spur on the next action and so on in a serial manner again.

However, an ambidextrous person, capable of operating with equal ability, using either hand or both the hands for that matter, may be able to manage this to a limited extent.

Here the mind also works in parallel operation orientation to be able to control the operation of both the hands which are engaged in the same activity.

It is to be noted here that contrary to the obvious thought, it is much more difficult to monitor and control the hands doing the same thing instead of the hands, which are engaged in disparate activity. Why so?

The intrinsic orientation of functioning of our two hands makes it imperative that these should operate in mirror image, if they are attempting the same functionality. This dissociation and counter operation mode of the two appendages makes it difficult for the mind to manage and impossible to sustain, if both the limbs are operating in the same orientation. To give an example, just sit on a chair, lift and rotate your left foot counterclockwise. Now lift your right foot and try to rotate it clockwise. See what I mean? This I can do easily.

Now try to rotate both feet counterclockwise or clockwise. This is difficult! Get it? Great! So, now we can move on to close associations and distant relationships that may be dissociated in a specific context.

The point I am making here is that the mind controls the body and is master of it. This is a fact that cannot be ignored or negated. What we are looking at, at this time, is the interaction of the relationships. How about starting with a relationship of the thorn and the rose? Is this another story of the beauty and the beast? Children's stories, we are definitely not targeting. If this serious effort of mine is mistaken for the children's stories; it will only amuse me, because that is the theme of my next book.

We are looking at the literal flower and the thorn that is its protector. It almost saves the flower this time also, from being plucked to become a part of the lifeless bouquet when it pricked the finger of the person collecting the long stemmed roses for a bouquet for the chief guest.

 Apparently the thorn was unsuccessful in its brave effort but did the rose know of the effort made by its gallant protector that has now been removed by being cut away from the stem by use of a heartless tool that announced and perpetrated the demise of the unsung hero.

The important issue here is that of the protected entity, the much admired rose, remaining completely unaware of close, yet seemingly distant love of thorn that has been its brave and committed protector knight for all this time.

The fact that feelings and attachment of the thorn have remained unacknowledged does not really matter in the larger scheme of events, as the affiliation of the thorn is at a different plane of cognizance.

This awareness and recognition is not beholden to the appreciation of audience or even the recognition of effort by protected entity, the rose, which is completely unaware of all the confusion and bedlam all around it.

This is the way of the rose. It feeds on nutrients needed to blossom from the ground and the manure.

When the rose achieves its glory of the full blossom, in its prime it easily forgets all those, who have contributed to its well-being and beauty and actually neglects them all. Actually this last statement may not be true at all.

I think that the rose remembers the contribution of all and not only does not acknowledge any of this but instead of acknowledging the effort of the supporting members, it carefully and deliberately distances itself from all those, who contributed to its success of being crowned with glory, lest they cast a shadow upon the expressed beauty and may try to claim some part of the credit.

We all know that the contributors are all fully satisfied with the rose being crowned and are happy for the achievement, but the rose cannot take risk of the limelight being shared. So, it shuns and distances them all, especially those, who helped and contributed to put the rose on the high pedestal.

This is the way of the Rose

The achievement of the rose is complete in itself, in standalone mode, without needing the support of perspective and crutches of the performance of other actors that can vary from performance to performance or even act to act and may hold hostage the narrative, which actually is a complete swan song in itself.

Another great love story for history books and literary compilations but a sad demise of the feeling of love in living times, once again. I really do have a serious reservation about love stories that end in a tragedy, as all great love stories do, probably with an aim to highlight the trait of sacrifice that strengthens all narratives.

On the other end of the spectrum we have a block of jaggery and the large black ant. The attraction of the jaggery exercises a pull that gets large black ant to traverse huge distances (in its own perspective) to reach the jaggrey block, to partake of the tasty morsel that is its prize for locating the block of jaggery.

Here we see that the brain is exercising its ability to produce and maintain myriad views of the thoughts that concern us in ways that we come to understand only when we reference and experience them all concurrently.

Let me give you another example. This is a simple one, much like others mentioned earlier and hereafter, which I shall also claim to be simple.

Stand with your right shoulder and the side of your right foot touching the wall. Now try to lift your left foot. You cannot do it without moving your right shoulder or the right foot because the equilibrium center of the brain, which gets its inputs from the otolithic membrane, located in the vestibular apparatus of inner ear and plays an essential role in brain's interpretation of equilibrium, senses in this action, a probable loss of equilibrium and blocks the attempt, even though logical thinking tells us that lifting of left foot with the right shoulder getting support from the wall is no cause of concern, in terms of maintaining balance of the body.

This is the power of the mind that it can exercise not only complete control but can also countermand the logic of its own deductive reasoning to issue overriding instructions, which may even be in conflict with the well-entrenched and proven norms and practices that have been defined by the mind itself, in an earlier context.

Daunted by the unlikely prospect of an iota of ephemeral happiness visiting my life, all the sorrows come together, in an unprecedented show of solidarity, to entrench themselves in my life with renewed commitment, so that they do not lose their rightful grip on my existence

MATURITY

'We, ourselves, have to be the change that we wish to see in the world'

The mind thinks many thoughts, leading us in different directions. No wonder there is so much chaos in the mind, creating serious traffic jams and even a few accidents!

Now imagine the state of the roads if we didn't have any traffic controlling mechanisms! So, what's needed is a traffic control system for our mind, which is what the maturity is all about.

Maturity of the thought has a lot to do with thought process itself. We need to define the maturity of thought; as in this scenario, we find ourselves marooned in the vista of acute scarcity of existing material to take advantage of. This is indeed, an impoverished era, devoid of the gift of fertility and richness. This age has inherited serious poverty of need addressing in all domains including thought.

I propose to define maturity as ripening or the coming of age of thought. We have addressed genesis and evolution and have seen fruition and growth of fruit to a fully developed stage. Now we come to the stage where we need to look at the ripening process of this fruit.

As always, we have a plethora of short cut options available. However, being perfectionists that we are, we shun these options of artificial fruit ripening that could have allowed us to realize the desired effect in less time and with a lot less effort. We also recognize the fact that all shortcuts may be fraught with plethora of problems that we may not be able to take cognizance of, at this time and in this context.

We have chosen natural ripening or maturity that encompasses all measures available to us to target the desired objective of maturity and we shall be rewarded for our effort and patience with the promise of enticing fragrance and fulsome taste of the naturally ripe fruit that invites partaking of. The obvious question is, why are we talking of the promise of reward and not the reward itself?

How can we forget that all reality is perception and even sensory inputs are deliberate illusions? You cannot touch illusions; any such act or the attempt thereof, shall result in premature crumbling of the edifice upon itself. We also must keep in perspective that the final stage of maturity is right next to and rubbing shoulders with cessation of existence event.

The final level of maturity achieved just before end of being, is legacy of the next generation. We cannot deny the inheritance, which is birthright of next generation and we are actually only the temporary keepers of this wealth of knowledge that is bequest of the next generation of inheritors.

We only have the assigned duty to protect and nurture this heritage, of which we are mere ephemeral custodians. Now I have to launch into the main thrust of my theory, which attempts to address the daunting task of defining that, which does not allow any definition or refuses to fit into any pattern.

The singularity that I attempt to address has no beginning or end. It is the ever new, yet also the oldest entity. It is the one entity that refutes all known rules and even the essentials of existence and cannot be known through sensory perception or through knowledge.

It is font of all wisdom but cannot be known through all the knowledge and wisdom, bestowed in all entities of the universe even in a combined and aligned form that realizes utmost synergy. No intellect can ponder upon it, no reason can touch it and no logic can help decipher it. This singularity is all pervading, omnipotent, omniscient and omnipresent, yet this eludes touch and permits no interpretation.

The fact is that what (or is it whom?) we are trying to know is beyond cognition of ordinary mortals like us and actually we should give ourselves a medal just for thinking of making an attempt towards this onerous task, which is the single most important quest of all the time gone by, the present and all time to come. So, why are we wasting our time in this bewildering maze of gigantic proportions where even the wise and well equipped have had to turn back empty handed?

This relates to the basic instinct of the pertinacious effort that allowed us to populate the planet and perpetuate our race. To keep on making an effort is in our genome and we are only letting it have a free rein. Here, I wish to include a story of blind men and the elephant, with a single minded purpose to illustrate that the perceptions can be highly misleading, if these are not viewed in the context of the overall perspective that gives definition to the heterogeneous assembly of disparate observations.

Four blind men came upon an elephant and were told that the animal is an elephant. These blind men tried to use the sense of touch to understand what an elephant is. This example attempts to showcase the fallibility of the blind that can be transmuted to fit the perspective of those, who can see but are still blind.

First blind man touching the leg of the elephant described it as a pillar. The second one touching the trunk said that it is like a flexible pipe. The third person touching the tail described the elephant as a rope. The fourth person, who touched the ear of elephant, likened the pachyderm to a huge fan.

The message here is that all of us, blinded by our own beliefs & conceits very quickly arrive at reasonable assumptions that make it easier for us to reach a destination that may be a total antithesis of our desired goal. It takes time to reach such understanding, which only happens after multiplicity of failures that, what we are attempting is impossible and we need to look for alternative methods and need to seek such patronage that can enlighten us to banish the lack of awareness.

Do we have available the alternatives that have a hope of making a dent in the walls of Jericho that confront us?

What we hope to try is to bring together all the questing souls in a super organism that can probably provide the needed tools and lead us to the objective.

This effort is also doomed to failure but we cannot help make another effort as we are genetically engineered to do, in the larger scheme of things including but not limited to perpetuation of human race on this planet.

This, I think is the right time to introduce the topic of truth itself as this is as good a time as any for this introduction and anyway I have to perform this obligatory responsibility sooner or later. This topic, which we are about to discuss has cast its shadow on the major part of the discussion that we have accomplished so far and I am sure, will continue to haunt us in the discussion hereafter also.

The topic of truth is such an all-encompassing feature that I hesitate to induct it without having created the required perspective for it, but then we have to do certain things as and when they should be done in alignment with the demands of the time.

Sometimes, it is a good idea to keep the snarling hounds at bay by maintaining a respectable distance. At other times, it may actually be a good idea to give the devil its due and get rid of it altogether.

I do think that this is one of those other times, when we should let it (the truth) have the center-stage and be done with it, even if only to get rid of its ever present shadow persona, which is ever ready to raise the conscience flag at all times.

It is not a new thought in the current context for me, but actually an earlier compilation that I reuse due to the demands of context.

Here goes:

TRUTH

Truth, ever is, a silent bystander, which eludes touch, refuses acceptance, rejects participation, recoils away from the need to stay in touch with reality; to remain true.

• What I cannot touch, cannot be the truth

• What I cannot feel, cannot be the truth

• This truth that has stayed beyond the tainted edges, a reasonable definition that we accept Just because we do not understand it, most definitely cannot be what we seek and search for – together

- Truth cannot be that reasonable

- Anything this much reasonable cannot be the truth

- Thin transparent sheets of time weld together to form opaque time frames that allow only whispers and shadows to pass through

- Truth need not be loud

- Truth may not always be serene

- Truth certainly will not be to our liking all the time

- Do we have the strength to deal with the truth?

- Do we deserve the truth?

- Truth is what we may have lost

- Truth is what may have gone by

- We may have passed it in an instant of time without realizing that we were faced with the truth

- We may choose to reflect the truth in to future in a hope that we may be able to catch up with it once more in the future, which may allow us a larger window of time to look at and address the issue

- However the tools to achieve the intended are fun mirrors; look - how twisted, how warped, how maimed the truth is, in this lost perspective

- Truth has serious affinity to its time frame and without the time stamp of the defining moment that lends the character to it, at this point in time; it loses its truth persona, its perspective

- Truth belongs; it cannot be ignored, projected away or escaped from

- Truth has a right to be harsh, and may not even find acceptance among the self-appointed keepers of the truth

- Truth is not a static entity; it is an evolving statement

- Truth is aware of the perspective

- Truth is in tune with the time

- Truth comes with the time stamp, which has validity

- Truth may not have an expiry date but it does become excess baggage over a period of time

- Truth is dynamic – perception dependent

"There are fundamental truths that lie at the bottom, the basis upon which a great many others rest, and in which they have their consistency. These are teeming truths, rich in store, with which they furnish the mind, and like the lights of heaven, are not only beautiful and entertaining in themselves, but give light and evidence to other things that without them could not be seen or known." - Locke

I must admit that it took me some time to work out this one. So, as is my custom, I leaned upon ancient wisdom of Hindu scriptures, the Vedas, to find an acceptable and far more important, a comprehensive answer.

This is what I came across that fits the discussion and delivers us from the dilemma that we straddle like horns of a rampant bull, which holds us captive with an all-encompassing intensity.

"Satyam bruyaat, priyam bruyaat;

naa bruyaat satyam apriyam"

Speak the truth, speak what is pleasant and refrain from speaking the unpleasant truth.

However, this dictum may not be misconstrued to mean that unpleasant truth should be suppressed. This is definitely not the case. This adage only permits us to defer the unpalatable truth, till it demands it's due.

This also presents a case for our consideration that there is a proper time and place for everything, even truth. The time and the space perspectives claim their due, as always, and cannot be denied.

Fact is that the truth can hurt.

Truth can indeed be damaging in certain perspectives. Why do doctors refrain from telling the terminal cancer patients that they may have only a limited time to live?

The fact is that knowing that I am living on borrowed time does not in any way alleviate my suffering or even prepare me for the end that may be coming soon. It may even damage the last vestiges of my courage to live.

The remnants of the will to live, with which I am hanging on to life with my finger nails may get washed away and make me succumb to the fact that the death is inevitable and I cannot do anything about it. This emphasis on our hapless state is definitely not a positive utterance.

This realization of helplessness cannot be of positive significance in any context, I can think of. In this context I wish to present you with the inevitable questions:

Would it be feasible for everyone to handle the truth?

Can everybody face the truth under all circumstances?

Whether everyone deserves the truth?

We escape from one dilemma and find ourselves immersed still deeper in another. This time the water is already over the head. Who will decide whether or not a person deserves the truth?

I do not want this rigorous responsibility on my slender shoulders that may not support this onerous philosophical burden. So I take the easy way out and leave the decision to the practitioners.

Practitioners also need support of a tool and it will be remiss on my part not to provide the sword of matador when I send them in to the arena before a raging bull. So the easy way out again. We choose half-truth. This may be easy for us, seasoned campaigners, but the amateurs are likely to be still found all at sea, even with this lifeline.

Half-truths, as you may have correctly guessed comprise both truth and lies. Truth singular and lies plural. That is what the game plan is. That is what it is going to be, because this is the only thing that works and is not required to be fixed in short term perspective. Though the implications of long term perspective still bother me but that is not here and now and I need to get some breathing space in this overbearing scenario.

I can live with it at this time. Future holds the key to addressing today's challenges, while the root cause of today's problems is in the past. The challenge is to keep the head high, eyes clear and the mind focused.

Do we have the energy and nerve to accept this challenge? It is to be ensured that we ourselves do not get lost in the hypnotic labyrinth of half-truths skillfully woven with mesmeric concoctions of partial truths. It is indeed easy to forget our way in this maze and lose the perspective. The real problem arises when we start getting proud of our skill in this arena and start believing in what we offer to others. We must at all times be aware of the distinction and also keep in perspective the fact that truth, as ever, remains the ultimate option.

The path of truth is easy as there is only one version; whereas the partial truths not only overlap but also at times can be indistinguishable from one another. Our persistent effort to keep the house of cards standing is surely a difficult proposition in these challenging circumstances. Do we have the necessary skill to keep it in place? Do we have the ability to keep afloat in the face of the raging storm that a crumbling half-truth is analogous to?

The very notion of half-truths is akin to cheating, which is inherently taxing to the conscience. The half-truths tend to breed cynicism in ourselves and others and lead to erosion of trust that has taken us a lot of time and effort to build.

Faith is a commodity that is scarce in our times and it should be dedicated endeavor of all of us to save it from all too frequent causes of attrition and finally extinction of this endangered species. Let me give you a powerful tool. This indeed is a litmus test. Just ask yourself; if and when the truth in its entirety comes out, do you expect the other people to thank you for your consideration of not telling them the complete truth earlier?

However, if this is not enough or not considered practical in the current perspective, I do have another arrow to my bow.

This involves asking yourself, whether you would give your associates, the authority, not to tell you the complete truth free of extraneous information, if they feel that this may not be appropriate at this time, to be brought to your attention and for your kind consideration.

It is to be clearly understood that it is not the answers that we may necessarily be seeking but at this time we just might only be interested in developing and enriching the question bank that will, in time, surely impress upon us to pursue the issue with persistent and tenacious efforts to gain the answers.

However, we must be prepared to accept the fact that some or all of these answers may be another set of questions and that we may have only succeeded in digging deeper and advancing steadily towards the ultimate answers that shall be derived from within. As and when we do look inwards, are we really likely to find the ultimate reality that we are seeking?

Sorry, this question does not relate to the subject, as this monumental search for ultimate reality is not covered under the topic currently under discussion. So we put this question on the parking lot and await the time when this query can be addressed.

Please do note the choice of word here. I have deliberately said addressed and not a more comprehensive answered. This care is taken because I am not sure that this query can even be addressed by the people, we are likely to encounter in our entire life time.

To lie or not to lie is the simple question that begs a simple answer. This simple answer is that:

One should not resort to lies, ever

The complex response rendered in simple terms forces us to consider the fact that, what we have labeled untruth today, needs to be researched, to find if it is not the truth, after all.

An advice of caution here; do we intelligent people really can make such a mistake where truth is labeled a lie and vice-versa?

I do admit that this is an unlikely occurrence but at the same time we need to address the fact that there may be such an eventuality when we are faced with unlikely situations that take a definite toll on a person and cloud the vision. I do think that Mark Twain got it right when he suggested that:

"When in doubt speak the truth. It will confound your enemies and astound your friends" **- Mark Twain**

Do not search for the answers outside, look inside where you are more likely to find them.

You shall find a kind of humbling greatness that fits our perspective.

This approach also permits us to enable a humble beginning to soar in to a gargantuan enterprise that even the founding members may not recognize and may find difficult to come to terms with.

Such is power of thought that it releases the latent energy stored within us, which at all times seeks an outlet to bloom in to a spectacular coruscation that helps us to realize all the targeted results with efficiency of optimal utilization of resources.

It is surprising that how solutions eventually come around for the most difficult problems that may have been labeled beyond solution at one time. There is a small trick to this unfathomable phenomenon.

We do not look for a solution; we do not try to find it.

What logic is this? Will the solution just decide to fall in my lap, if I stop thinking about it? Of course it will. Remember the old time tricks like *'sleep over a problem' and also* 'take a break-think afresh'.

However I have a still better solution.

Try to remember the solution, as if we have solved the problem earlier.

Let me introduce you to Buddhist way of recollecting. This method enables us to tap in to the plethora of information stored in the subconscious mind and pops up the solution as if it was there in front of our eyes all the time, while we were searching for it. It is just a thought that is worth a try.

A spectacular hunch

As per Buddhist scriptures if we are able to concentrate strongly enough and long enough, other than our own mind, we can also access the super set of consciousness, knowledge and reason. Let us hope that this will serve the purpose.

Alas, this also does not measure up. How do I know this to be unsuccessful when I am only a detached external observer? Oh yes, I do. If this had worked, we would not still be here but would have declared a wrap up and would have been relaxing with ice cold beer cans in hand, in a quiet green meadow.

Now we are left with the only weapon at our command left to be tried. This is the method that tries to establish what it is not and by using this exclusion extensively to separate the remainder which may be our objective. This actually is one of the ancient Hindu philosophy techniques of reason and logic. The method is to arrive at the conclusion by using exclusion to the very limits. This is called 'Neti, Neti' technique of reason. Literally, this it is not, this it is not, to be exercised till we are left with only what it is.

This surely is a roundabout manner but an effective one nevertheless. This is particularly useful here, because the singularity can only be reasonably approximated by keeping on excluding, what it is not. In this context, even what it is not, also may be subject to reasonable approximation based on preconceived notions that may or may not be correct, relevant or applicable.

In this treatise I seem to be bent upon making a lot of radical statements. Here is another:

The highest degree of maturity of thought, actually is, _Thoughtlessness_

What we are saying is that a mature thought is nothing. This assertion may lead some of us to an assumption that a mature thought does not exist. This is surely not the case, at least in this perspective here.

The mature thought, in this scenario, may get manifested in reality and cease to be a thought, hence the absence of thought. This is still not satisfactory.

So what do we do? We keep searching, looking for the elusive answer, as always. Please allow me to put forward another hypothesis. Maturity of a thought signifies that the thought has realized all the answers needed to satisfy the questions raised by it. Hence, the thought is no longer in a questing mode. Actually this mature thought is now at peace with itself and is resting peacefully in Yoga-Nidra.

The thought that is peaceful has no unrequited query that could have kept it restless. This is the much talked about state of thoughtlessness. We were not talking about absence of thought at all. Even when we sleep, our mind is not free from the quest for answers for unrequited queries and the only way to achieve a peaceful form is to satisfy all queries.

We have talked about singularity till now, but we do recognize the existence of duality in a transient form. Let us consider this as supreme conscious and a multitude of ordinary beings. To narrow the spectrum, so as to keep it manageable, let us talk of one super conscious being, which is representative of the multitude.

The next step is to say that this representative being of the multitude is a dissociated extension of supreme conscious and only appears to have a separate form and identity. Let us further state that this super conscious being, at a later time, will surely be re-assimilated in to the supreme conscious entity. So, after a lot of run around, we are finally left with the singularity we had started with, when we started to dwell on this topic.

The only difference discernible to the wise is that, we started with a young thought that has now attained maturity; although, there may not be a discernible change of form of the thought to clearly signify the change.

At one time or the other, actually time and again, we are faced with the vicissitudes of the life, which present to us in a never-ending stream, the little conundrums of life that challenge us to seek gratification for the endless quest that leads us to a point in time, when and where we must seek answers for the essential questions that face us inexorably and petition us to seek insight in to enigma that cajoles us to take a stand for what we express belief in.

It is much more important to take care of, or at least engage, the small, less significant items in the complex labyrinth of copious issues vying vociferously for attention.

The big and important things of life, this includes work life, are more likely to be taken care of by us or even by someone else, due to the plethora of urgent flags attached to these, but we must not allow the little niceties to take a back seat initially and then be ignored altogether due to the missing attention flags that scream importance.

These **'little things'**, a misnomer of a title, may also include all such items that we tend to take for granted, which may include even important issues by oversight or for convenience, by those of us, who, due to lack of capability or understanding do not wish to grapple with the issue, till it becomes urgent and of such proportions that it no longer can sustain the 'little thing' label. This issue actually questions and puts to test our inherent discerning ability, which is the hallmark of a learned thinker and forces us to revisit the classification criteria afresh.

To give an example from everyday life, let us take a scenario where I invite some people for a meal, but fail to inquire and provide for the special needs of the invitees. When I invite families, I must provide for needs and sometimes for wants also, of the young people. I also cannot club teenagers and toddlers in the same group and consider the job done. This is a sure recipe for disaster, as these uncared-for wants may test our flexibility and capacity for accommodating the needed dynamic change in this scenario. Similarly, when there is a formal signing of an agreement between two nations, we may not assume that people will carry their own writing implements and I must provide for the writing instruments.

My rest room for handicapped people is not always in perfect state of repair, as it is not used at all. This is not acceptable, as I do not wish to land in to a problem, when I have a handicapped visitor. Small things matter a lot, little things such as support rails in a stair-well.

A lot of thinking goes into providing for these small items of need that may only be required rarely, but when needed it is not the availability but the lack of it, that registers.

There are other small things also, like mentioning your own name, or prominently displaying your name tag. This actually helps a person, who knows you well but is unable to dredge up your name from the memory.

This act of being nice may never get verbally acknowledged or appreciated but the value of the act is very much there to observe and savor as the person visibly relaxes and is likely to be kind and attentive to you in the immediate future interaction, which is the integral part of the scheme and purpose of the interaction.

If you are a senior and/ or well-known person in your profession, this act enhances your perceived humbleness and positively contributes to your stature. This is likely to be perceived as an expression of humility on your part.

This small act of mentioning your name may get you an extremely favorable response, such as 'thank you madam/ sir, we all know you', or may be an even more flattering expression 'who, in our profession does not know you madam/ sir'. We have touched upon thoughtlessness earlier in the transcript, but now we look at this concept from the perspective of maturity of thought.

When we look at the final level of maturity of thought as thoughtlessness, it does sound a bit confusing but this is what we intend to look at, so I must include a little detail here, so that the concept can be explained in somewhat simpler terms with the purpose of enabling understanding and assimilation.

Focused meditation is the path; we are leading you to, at this juncture; so I need to add a foretaste of the same to address the seemingly obvious incongruity that threatens to acquire unmanageable proportions, if left unaddressed.

What we are looking at here, is the concept of focusing all our energies without any permitted deviation or diversion, which may compromise our focus and render the whole exercise useless. This concerted focus on a single thought point is what we intend to achieve as the first step towards attempted thoughtlessness.

When we achieve this aim of focusing our full faculties on the issue under contemplation, we target the outcome of a single thought occupying our mind, with a purpose of resolving the issue in a single-task oriented approach.

This approach does not free us from the grip of associated thoughts, related to the issue/ thought being contemplated but is helpful nevertheless.

For example, when I perceive the unavoidable certainty of a head–on collision with another vehicle coming from opposite direction, in that instant, all the mental faculties are concentrated on the single purpose of avoiding this impact, which I manage with inches to spare. The shivers that grip me now, are just the manifestation of realization of escape from certain death at this time.

Now, I sit in my vehicle stopped on the shoulder of the road, shivering, as the physical reaction sets in. At the time when I was thinking and planning to avoid the impact with a single minded commitment, I achieved a split second concentration on a single thought.

Then the physical reaction took over and the split second concentration on single thought was over exactly at the instant, when the physical reaction took over. However, please note that the mind did not let go off the thought completely, when it shifted from the mode of planning and evaluating the alternatives at the extreme edge of our abilities and moved to observation mode.

This is the instant, we wish to concentrate upon, when our mind, so completely occupied with most important concern of preserving life, moves from the state of evaluating alternatives and decision making for optimal course of action targeted at preserving life, the most important consideration, second only to perpetuation of the race in general and own family line in particular. We need to concentrate on and recognize this moment as the highly important instant, defining the change of state.

This instant of shifting of the focus is important to us, as this is a fleeting moment of zero thought status of the mind, we so assiduously seek and attempt to recognize.

The focus now moves from decision orientation to observation orientation with a purpose to correct the selected option, if it does not seem to serve the purpose of attaining the objective of self-preservation. Now the mind can safely move into purely observation mode with the best available alternative and dynamic corrective action, if applicable, put in action.

This instant of changeover from thinking/ evaluating/ deciding to physical action is the defining moment and in this scenario of life threatening circumstance, we may encounter a fleeting moment of thoughtlessness when the mind is completely unoccupied.

This is immediately followed by the continual flash of all the important events in life of the person in a pictorial representation, irrespective of whether the crash is averted or we are still on the path of unavoidable impact, which will probably be the end of our life, as we know it.

At this stage the concept of soul comes in handy and provides us with an unfathomable feeling of being in control of the events of life and beyond.

The soul is unaffected by demise of physical body and gets assimilated in the supreme consciousness entity, to be lent a physical form again in the context of an upcoming birth, which represents arrival of a new mind that may provide the medium for the object thought to be held for the purpose of being worked upon for a period of time that can be sustained by the physical body occupied by the thought under contemplation.

We were in an unexpressed form before birth and get manifested as a human body only for a short duration, actually an infinitesimal time period in the cosmic scheme of events, to become unexpressed again upon death, which only represents a change of state and dissolution of the acquired and developed associations, which may have an attribute that can compromise contemplation of the thought being ruminated upon.

This is nothing cataclysmic but only a change of state in the complex intertwined relationship state between the body and the soul, which many a time is labeled beyond understanding for ordinary mortals like us. So, we must not grieve but immediately take up the task of planning for development of the mind which is integral part of the body, in which the soul has taken up temporary residence.

The purpose is that, this new mind can take up further contemplation from the point at which it was interrupted earlier, in an analogous but distinctly separate continuum.

In alignment with the infinite wisdom of the Chinese immortal chow kok koh, let me state that we are put on the earth to build character and it is adversities that shape our character, affecting the visible components as to how we behave and perform. We must understand that this expression is only a small visible portion of the whole, contemplating which, is definitely beyond our limited abilities.

This current edition of the universe is a collective expression of assimilated thoughts of all the beings that comprise it. We may wish to include the extraterrestrial beings also here for good measure with the aim of developing an all-inclusive doctrine.

The unicellular organisms are occupied only with the single thought of dividing and multiplying, thereby contributing the only thought at this consciousness level, which is that of perpetuation and propagation of the race that is represented by them.

Moving up the evolution pyramid, we encounter, at the apex, the human being endowed with an ability to think, contemplate and act for the benefit of and in the interest of self, society and the universe at large.

This is one thought that separates the higher intelligence from the lower order of intelligence including but not limited to the primitive ones.

As we move up the evolution pyramid, we encounter thoughts that are increasingly complex and involve byzantine intertwining that defines the interrelationships, which are core strength of the highly evolved mind that maps to human beings.

Knowing what we know and what we do not is a very important aspect of intelligence and is labeled Meta-knowledge. Meta-knowledge, the analytical ability, compassion and the interrelated thought map along with ability to multitask with defined prioritization are some of the myriad things that make the human mind stand out.

This, in itself, is a distinction sufficient enough, between the primitive and the evolved mind but now that we have touched upon the issue, we might as well dwell further on this topic. Some of the other characteristics of an evolved mind are comprehension of relational logic and the ability to segregate the grain from the chaff (essential from residual). This is labeled discerning ability, which is an integral part of the repertoire of a responsible thinker.

Many a time, when we forget something, we can easily recollect it, if at one point of time our mind had worked on analyzing the information bit to establish relational connects. The open, free floating synapse links force a reconstruct that fits the logical pattern and the resulting construct is almost exactly the same or so akin to the lost information bit, so as to align the viewer thoughts to look for similarities instead of differences.

This rebuilding of information, using the relational threads, is at the core of the lost information recovery mechanisms, used by modern computers. This actually has high consanguinity with the neural synapses re-orientation that is a continual activity, which occupies the brain.

These relational links that re-orient to support new thought models are the very basis of generation of offshoots, which are genesis of new thoughts in the same thought space and get linked in a complex manner to existing thought constructs, to give them additional or even completely new interpretations, in the dynamic tapestry of interwoven active thought patterns.

Surprisingly, some of these new constructs may even be inimical to previously held opinion/ thought and are likely to be called upon to face the inquiry that is the test by fire, which every new thought has to go through and this proven endurance confers upon the subject thought, the much sought after acceptability and approval of the group. This method has an obvious built-in contradiction that may at some point or the other, result in a situation of confrontation as a consequence. Confrontation is never a good mode to operate in, as this gives rise to anger, which indeed is a difficult emotional thought to deal with, in all the conceivable perspectives and at all times.

Emotional aspect of thought only deals with the feeling and the effect of it, as the genesis of strong emotional thoughts, such as jealousy, envy and false pride, in another set of confrontational thoughts that portend no good for the involved individuals and result in stretching to the limits of the societal norms and relationship bonds, which even within a close-knit family, may get burdened at times, with the emotional encumbrance so brought upon.

How to deal with it? Especially when the matter is within the immediate family? The proven technique proposed here is to use the technique of 'smile and silence'.

A smile to solve the problems

Silence to avoid the problems

These simple tools when employed judiciously enable effective solutions to many a problem that have a potential to blow up in to major issues, which may eventually snowball in to problems, big enough to test the social fabric and at times, even threaten its breakdown.

This, actually, is the test of our mettle. Suggestions are all here; how we deploy them will shape the outcome. Onus is upon us to act with care, compassion and elegance.

Human beings are essentially social animals. It may not be an overstatement to say that we are actually afraid of being lonely. This leads us to a conclusion that we will do everything in our capacity, not to be banished from the society as an outcast. Sometimes, this may involve an agreement with the group thought, even when we wish to disagree, as the general consensus may not always be in alignment with our own deeply held beliefs, which guide and shape the formulation of our thoughts.

This almost forced alignment that holds sway over our preconceived notions is an important aspect that needs to be looked in to. Just think of a scenario where everyone does things in accordance with the long established practices that have almost become regulations, which govern our conduct and external expressions of our thoughts.

Please permit me to draw your attention to the fact that here we are looking at an stagnant environment that has no hope of progress and can only regress and contributes only to rent the social fabric with lacerations that cannot be mended and may even cause the society to fall apart.

To move ahead and progress we need to look at alternatives, ponder upon them and if these are found suitable, implement the same for benefit of the co-existent group. Now, the thought to be pondered upon is, where do these new ideas come from? Innovative ideas always come from the minds that are as yet free from the clutter of the inhibitions and have not yet been influenced by the perceived sanctity of the boundaries.

These may come from the section relegated to minority that has not been able to get a hearing or even a lone voice that may, by proxy represent our group conscience, biding its time to be heard and may be the radical change that alters the complete identity of the civilization, time and again to prove that everything is liable to change. In the bygone era, it may have been difficult to think of fire as a useful thing, till the time, someone tried to roast the raw meat, which was the staple till that time. Invention of wheel also must have made drastic changes in the social functional pattern, which may have settled in a comfortable zone of status quo, resisting all change.

It is same for the introduction of bronze and so on. I could go on endlessly but I think that I can safely assume that there is no need for it.

The lack of situational awareness promotes traditional processes and strengthens the regressive attitude that dictates preference for the status quo, which strangulates the progressive thought and guillotines innovation

Radical thoughts, as if by design, do not evolve from consensus but need a lone warrior, who takes up the cudgels and shows necessary courage and application to prove the effectiveness of new idea, tool or device.

'A revolutionary thought, time of which has arrived, is the most powerful force in the universe.'

"The reasonable man adapts himself to the world; the unreasonable one persists to adapt the world to himself. Therefore all progress depends on the unreasonable man" - *George Bernard Shaw.*

Now, let me introduce the devil's advocate reasoning and highlight its usefulness. All the new thoughts need to be subjected to this abrasive facet of thought evaluation. This is necessary, because new inventions can also be of the genre of atomic bomb, which can wreak major havoc. It may have had its limited purpose in a certain context, as held by the multitudes serving in the pacific theater of WWII, who suffered from the most inhuman expression of the oriental wrath.

Till the time, such forces are tamed and are offered for use in a controlled operational implementation mode of the safe atomic reactors that provide low cost energy option; the destructive tag shall remain operative.

Every new idea needs time to prove its usefulness and such needed time, in my opinion should be allowed, if we wish to assure ourselves of the efficacy of safety devices to ensure the sufficiency of the safeguards.

A case in perspective is the catastrophe in the island nation of Japan that has once again put center stage, the destructive ability of unbridled atomic monster that perpetrated mayhem, in spite of the unprecedented show of solidarity and honor of the call of duty, even in face of personal harm, which is the hallmark of Japanese people.

This also puts in proper perspective, service by the people much beyond call of duty in face of grave personal peril for benefit of the greatest good for the greatest numbers of people. At such times of extreme stress, there is a probability that misunderstandings may also occur.

We must deal with these issues, for these are born out of warped perception and not as a work of some ill-intentioned lout or a half- wit, retarded moron, who just wakes up to the perceived call of duty and lets loose the opprobrium in a reckless tirade.

To clear the air of a misunderstanding; before you speak, choose the right environment, and work out how far you are prepared to go in the interests of good relations and then go a step further. Communicate your feelings. Be open and honest. Be generous and kindhearted.

An honest expression of the inner feelings can never go wrong. Unconditional apology is usually a good starting point, even if the fault does not attach to us. The other person will appreciate your generosity and also you, even if there is no verbal acknowledgment and/ or expression of the same.

Motivation and enthusiasm are also trying to force their way in to the discussion, so let us permit them to make an appearance, as such important entities cannot be denied their due for long. These thoughts have both individual and group perspectives and both these facets must be accorded their rightful place under the sun, which they justly deserve. In the individual orientation, lack of these, is both energy sapping and inaction feeding.

However, we must also be careful with overdose of these highly effective emotions, as an uncontrolled infusion may inadvertently result in a bloated ego, instead of serving the intended ego boost objective. Care must be exercised to ensure that humility continues to be an integral part of pride without which, the expression of pride may very quickly deteriorate in to unacceptable and unwarranted manifestation of conceit, which we must eschew at all times.

"Enthusiasm, which, though founded neither on reason nor divine revelation, but rising from the conceits of a warmed or overweening brain . . . men being most forwardly obedient to the impulses they receive from themselves . . . For strong conceit, like a new principle, carries all easily with it, when got above common sense, and freed from all restraint of reason." - Locke

We must, at all times, be still more careful when we apply these to the group entity as the same principles apply but the outcome gets manifested in an accentuated form that is expected of a powerfully aligned group entity.

Let us move on to a familiar discourse in the interest of retaining complete audience focus. I have this propensity of lapsing in to silence and a sort of reverie at times, which is highly disconcerting to people around me.

I actually added several blank pages just now that will get deleted during proof reading, so what is the point to mention this not-of-any-use information? This was just to give you a flavor of the discomfiture this induces in the people who have to suffer me and bear with me, day in and day out. I frequently get asked if I am all right. This is not an issue we will dwell upon now. The problem arises when people, especially my lady friends/ colleagues ask me if I am lonely.

I actually have friends; living, breathing, talking friends. So, all my friends please take note and never complain again that I never feature you in my books. It may look like that I am targeting the end of this book; not so at all. There is another full chapter on the seriously contentious issue of 'oblivion of the thought' after this one.

After all, it is not often that I get a captive audience; but when I do, like now, I do not let them off the hook, so easily. My way to explain to my colleagues, my frequent reveries, is to tell them that they are mistaken, as there is a significant difference between being alone and being lonely.

I may be alone, and I do wish to be alone for some time every day, preferably in the beginning of the work day to collect my thoughts and plan the day. I further mention:

Please understand that I am almost never lonely, for I have the best and most preferred company - me.

When we are asleep, our mind works to annotate and store the observations, occurrences and thoughts experienced during the day in a relational manner that facilitates efficient retrieval at later stage. What we remember, endows us with information; what we understand gives us knowledge and what we assimilate and learn from acquired experience and experienced thoughts, gives us wisdom.

Intelligent people learn from their own mistakes; a wise person learns from the mistakes of other people. This is a necessary device required to facilitate learning as we cannot commit all the mistakes ourselves and learn from direct experience, all the time. Some of you would be familiar with my proclivity to discuss sets of words and may think that I use this to fill up pages; this is not true.

I may actually be doing just that right now and try to lead you to think that this exercise has a solemn endowment of wisdom.

Two words at this time, Sanskrit words at that:

•Yoga

•Kshem

The word 'Yoga' literally means addition and we will just say that yoga means adding to what we already possess.

The other word is 'Kshem' and for the purpose of our discussion, we shall term it as *maintenance*. Maintenance of what we possess at this time. Please take note that maintenance includes upkeep of the current possessions and also implies upgrade of the same, as and when required, to keep our inheritance up to date and usable in the current context at all times. Now we shall look at a few practical applications.

A very simple exercise is controlled deep breathing, which is the very first step towards meditation. I will only be touching upon a few aspects of the much debated and intriguing topic of meditation only with a purpose to provide a stable platform for the thoughts being expressed and discussed in this discourse.

A full-fledged discussion on the intricate topic of meditation is beyond my limited knowledge and abilities and as I am fully aware of this certainty, I shall steer clear of this onerous responsibility; though, the intrigue of the topic fascinates me and the prospect of the captive audience is a definite temptation, but I turn my back on these temptations to chart a safe course that may not bring me quick results, but is likely to lead me to the promised land in a safe, sure and certain manner.

The process is simple. Inhale from one nostril and exhale out of the other. This has to be done following deliberate slow and deep breathing process; which we must be in control of; all the time. Inhale deeply and hold your breath for a time that you can manage without much stress. Initially, you may have to physically close one nostril while inhaling from the other and then physically close this nostril to exhale from the nostril that was closed physically during inhalation from the other nostril.

When we practice this for a reasonably long duration of time over a period of several days, at one time you may be surprised to find that now you can manage this inhalation from one nostril and exhalation from another nostril, without any need for forced physical closure of one of the nostrils turn by turn.

Then we alternate the inhaling and exhaling nostril and achieve complete control over this.

At this point, when we have achieved reasonable control over breathing process, we are now ready for the next step. Now exhale slowly in a continuous stream. The important part here is to be in control of the process of inhaling and exhaling. The trick here at this stage is, not to starve your lungs of oxygen in an extreme manner but to be in control of the breathing process.

Now is the time to reach for the next step. This calls for us to wait for a while before inhaling after complete exhalation has been achieved. This is the most important issue in this process, as in the normal exhalation part of the breathing process; we never exhale completely but only partially all the time.

When we try to wait a while after complete exhalation, our body starts to clamor for oxygen and this becomes a perceived life threatening issue and need for oxygen now becomes an urgent life continuation requirement, which overshadows all other thoughts and the mind is now focused on the need for oxygen with a single point agenda of such intensity that all other thoughts are banished from the mind to create a positive vacuum.

Now, we satisfy this single thought of high intensity urge, which has banished all other thoughts, by inhaling.

This satisfied thought, now reaches maturity, leaving behind a positive vacuum that enables us to achieve the state of thoughtlessness for a brief instant allowing us a glimpse at the eternity, which we have so assiduously sought and have achieved now. We now understand that all this buildup was intended to compel our mind to think that we are facing a life threatening situation and get our mind to concentrate on the agenda of saving life.

This derived focus helps to enable proscription of all other thoughts from our mind. This single point determination, which enables us to ostracize all other thoughts from the cognizable spectrum, is the key to achievement of the targeted objective.

Now, we inhale life sustaining air, full of oxygen needed by the body and then, this need satisfied with this simple act of inhalation, we are allowed a brief moment in time, of thoughtlessness that actually permits us a glance at the supreme consciousness, which was our aim to begin with.

Those enlightened people, who have been endowed with the ability to do so, or those who have acquired this ability by practice of this art with a single point resoluteness, may know, as to how to steal this moment from the continually moving stream of time for the purpose of serious contemplation at a later time with a single minded purpose of the knowledgeable interpretation by focused rumination.

This is not easy and there seems to a deliberate scheme about it also. The knowledge and wisdom are for the worthy and shall only be made available to deserving people, who have earned right of access to the hallowed portals of wisdom of the ages. A mature thought is a powerful entity that has the ability to alter the physical world.

A strong positive thought, exercising its full might changes the world for the better. A simple example is that, when we launch in to an initiative with certainty of positive outcome, the whole world plots to help us in our endeavor. Please note that a negative thought on the other hand may destroy or render useless all the ground work, accomplished in a proactive manner by us, towards the targeted goal.

We must understand that, if thoughts have power to change the world, then a positive thought that supports creation, always has a negative counterpart that may enable destruction. Therefore, we must be careful and alert to shun the negative thought, as all of us know that it is easier to destroy than to create. This is the main reason, which dictates that the knowledge may only be imparted to those, who have proven their worthiness for the cause. This may compromise the much advocated all-inclusiveness doctrine but the exclusion of probable irritants shall definitely have a positive effect on the end result.

The conscience:

The conscience is the inner core of the consciousness model that comprises several layers, which many a time may be mistaken to be packaging layers for the item of substance. It is to be recognized that the layers themselves are the essence or at least an integral part of the whole and an attempt of unraveling is surely not a sustainable enterprise. We make an attempt to remove the outer packaging to reach the core and then realize that in this quest, we have to take a note of everything and will be unable to move forward, if we make the cardinal mistake of discarding what we may have gained, in our mistaken belief, considered to be and labeled as peripheral to the central issue.

Outermost layer represents the anomalies that shall continue to occupy the periphery till a suitable place is found for them in the context of defined priorities aligned with the current equation.

The next inner layer represents the clarity and highlights the distinction of our doctrine. Our proposed school of thought may even have been targeted at trivial issues, as they may be perceived to be, at this time. This exercise helps to provide us with an opportunity to refine our thought construct in the pilot mode before finalization of the idea for full-fledged implementation.

The next layer deals with aesthetics and harmony with the environment, which we wish to present as our central theme. This set is relevant as this represents finer feelings, which are derived expression of our existence.

Still another inner layer deals with memory items, their retention, retrieval and update as a regular institutionalized activity that works in alignment with the selected algorithm to take care of the basic operations as a routine and neither requires regular intervention, decision making nor any special effort for convergent decision implementation.

Now we move on to the logic and reason that evaluates every item to establish the veracity, validity and relevance in the current scheme of events. Then, as next logical step we take up values and inhibition inheritance. Inhibitions may also have a positive effect sometimes.

The required decisions that deal with the value system are inherently taxing and may also demand us to make our stand clear on the core issues. This is an exercise that tests our resolve and puts urgent taxing demands on our intelligence, knowledge and discerning ability.

These are the capable thought constructs that guard our conscience, the inner awakening, which has a voice unencumbered with guile and shuns all subterfuges.

I wish to go back to the very strong emotion of fear once again. Now, we feel empowered enough to take up this challenge and get in to discussion of cause of fear.

What causes fear?

A prospect of death causes fear as it negatively affects our primal need for continuation of existence.

Please take a note that how clever I am. I have deliberately chosen an extreme example to frustrate your attempts to corner me. This scheme of events seems to be an ideal solution. The only 'fly in the ointment' is that in this crowd of voices, I forgot that I am the inquisitor also.

How can I forget that as established earlier in no uncertain terms, death is but a change of state and we need to satisfy this unrequited quest? So, the question is in the unaddressed, hanging-fire mode, till some clarity emerges. The main cause of fear is change. I can deal with this also. I again forgot that I am a tough interrogator. What is change?

Change is what threatens to and sometime even manages to get us out of our status quo of the Utopian existence. This, now, is troubling; we do not want to come out of the Utopian status quo and diligently resist all attempts to get us out of the bed on a chilly winter morning. This is the ever pleasant embrace of relaxed posture of peaceful slumber that cocoons us to the extent of our starting to get comfortable, in this tranquil sarcophagus to calmly await the end of days.

What causes change?

Change is brought upon by the passage of time that ushers in the new perspectives that are inimical to current state of existence and demand change.

So, what can we do?

Eliminate the root cause of the problem

Stop time!

I *stand here, holding the hands of the clock.*

Time is stopped; it cannot move now.

How much time have I wasted in this useless endeavor?

OBLIVION

Oblivion addresses the regression of thoughts and associated specific measures of the same. This thought here and now, deals with probably the best gift God has bestowed upon us.

Yes, I am indeed talking about the ability to forget.

This not only saves us from going mad, and also helps to clear the debris of outdated, useless and irrelevant thoughts, which are well past their expiry date in temporal aspect and should have been discarded as they have outlived their usefulness and must be excluded to streamline the thought-scape.

The thought-scape can now be easily reorganized, to enable mapping of remainder thoughts that have passed the test of time, with current spectrum and morphing demands of time and the current context in terms of geographical orientation and people centric approach, in psychological and physiological context that defines the cognizable domain.

I will leave you with this thought for the time being, as we need to discuss a few more items of importance, before we launch our foray in to the oblivion.

Thoughts are like ideas written on paper, which can be crumpled and thrown in waste paper basket. If we throw out an important idea and remember about it in time, we can actually retrieve the crumpled bit of paper, smooth it out and if we are lucky, which all people with a definite aim and purpose are, we can re-enter the idea in the context to which it belongs, or belonged, to begin with. This retrieval ability helps us to reconstruct the relevant scenario with an aim to utilize this for aggrandizement of the target objective.

The creases of time serve to further highlight importance of the idea, as it has now been re-acknowledged with definite re-iterated purpose that makes the once rejected thought, which is now adjudged to be both current and serviceable, now reinstated as the favored idea, which is ready to take its appointed place, among acknowledged luminaries of the refined thought set.

Now, with permission of the learned audience, I wish to pick up the thread from the point where we had chosen to defer it. I have been thinking about as to what exactly I am going to write in this section. The considered opinion that I have arrived at is not in conflict with my first thought about this issue, for which I am thankful.

It is time to admit that this whole text has not been written in a serial manner. Actually I started with writing a couple of pages intended to be a short essay and then I got a feeling that a lot more needs to be said on this topic and I myself can contribute a sizable amount. So, I decided on the nomenclature of the chapters in which I wish to segregate the discourse to give it the necessary focus, for the benefit of the audience and sufficient succinct think points for me to deliberate upon and expand it to a model that provides required elaboration and at the same time aims to also fulfill the primary requirement of being manageable, as an appreciable thought construct.

Let me not digress and try to remain with the core focus of thought oblivion. Thinking on this topic yielded three distinct thought points that can hold the fort on their own.

However, since I need to be definite, I shall choose one but request for the liberty to mention all three in a brief outlay, as it serves to build the perspective.

My first thought was that oblivion of the thought is its being pushed beyond the cognizable limits by employing the devices of obfuscation & mystification, to arrive at the confusion that heralds the demise of the idea, its oblivion, while retaining the premise that was its genesis, for further contemplation.

This actually, is the often used ploy that we replace the thought that is uncomfortable to us, by a similar looking thought that can even be an antithesis of the irritating thought being replaced.

The second option that caught my interest was that taking the thought to its obvious conclusion and then reading out eulogies in the obituary postscript would be an obvious choice, to qualify for being recognized as the oblivion of thought.

This indeed is an elegant solution but my first thought on this topic started sending out urgent reminders for recognition.

To reiterate the earlier stated alternative as the third option, let me state that forgetting a thought is its oblivion. So, how is it different from the first option of pushing the thought beyond cognizable boundaries? While the first option at least makes an attempt at deliberate action, forgetting is completely involuntary and perhaps beyond our control and sometimes the method itself may be beyond certain limits, as what we understand and interpret as voluntary action, may actually be a coerced attempt.

The ability to forget is a gift of God. Without this trait, we may end up with an unmanageable miasma of myriad thoughts that test our ability of cognizance to stretch limits of the cognizable spectrum and beyond.

Since forgetting is involuntary, though it follows defined postulates, it allows us to purge the thought burden, which we may have retained, if this was a voluntary activity in a controlled environment.

However forgetting is not entirely illogical. It is a specific process based on a defined algorithm, employing the logic of retaining the most accessed and also the most recently accessed information set.

The information set propounded here is defined by the relational linkages that determine the logic for retaining preference guided by linkage bonds to access count and access time stamp of the accessed information set, which depends upon the operational exigencies that are likely to be dynamic in nature.

The dynamic nature of this equation needs to be taken in to account and has to be catered for, in the larger scheme of events that demand such attributes to be taken cognizance of.

Next, we embark upon the onerous task of correlation and interpretation of thoughts in the relational space, which gives the thought construct its co-relational significance in the operating domain that defines the paradigm, in which this thought may have existential relevance. Now, let us look at some still more intriguing questions, as we give shape to our thoughts on this issue.

We are what we think. So, it can be established that our identity is shaped by our thoughts.

'I think, therefore I am'
'I know that I think, therefore I am'
'I know that I can think, therefore I exist'

Please note that simple statements are holding us captive once again and there is no escape as we have ourselves, helped to shape these axioms that trouble us now. It is not as if we expected the answers to be provided by someone else, but at the time of framing of the questions, I had a different hat on, that of the devil's advocate and now that we are back in our well-meaning operational role of a supportive facilitator, this is suddenly a difficult place to be in.

In these impolite times of relentless information overload, even the good thoughts have to fight for attention, in the incessant clamor that occupies us and in a moment of frustration, we may ask a good thought to await its turn to get in to our attention domain, as we find it difficult to accommodate all the requests for attention and in a moment of affected schedule constraint, we may not find the time to address an extraordinary idea immediately and ask it to wait, or even more reprehensible, ask it to go away.

The idea asks to be taken cognizance of, once, twice and then it goes away. How can it do that? It turns its back on us when we needed it most, though it keeps on disturbing us with its irritating presence, when we want some peace. All of them are traitors.

We are all busy and we have been taught the virtues of time management and the value of time. However, there are times, when we must find the time urgently to listen to a path-breaking idea that is not so labeled, as yet.

These are the times, when we must prioritize and make time for ideas, which deserve the time and defer other important activities to a less crowded place in time. Even if some items need to be dropped in face of the revised priority regime; we must be ruthless, as and when required.

Several other people of our ilk, brought up in the same demanding scenario, may promptly recognize importance of the idea and may ensure that they assign the requisite time for this highly innovative idea of great significance and we may be left out. The need is so great that we must find time for this indulgence.

There are times, when we do not get our priorities right and fail to respect the time element, which is the most important parameter and a crucial center stage factor in the final analysis and we may also not find the time to listen to a thought that does not fit the accepted patterns and transgresses time honored boundaries and preset limits of acceptable format.

The main problem is that I must account for the time used, in terms of value generation, which for the uninitiated, translates directly to money earned and must be given its due importance in the overall scheme of events. The message here is:

Value your time, but please do not put a price tag on it.

Do not be afraid of looking at thoughts that may not be relevant to current discussion. Sometimes, these unrelated thoughts, may be part of solutions that are needed to address problem issues, which are lurking on the periphery and we may only be aware of them at the subconscious level.

We need to understand that spending time on these issues is not a waste of time, but actually an investment for future, when cognizance of these issues, being deliberated now, will save us precious time, when we are under pressure to provide solutions to the problems that are yet to show up.

Our mind is the main stakeholder which influences and directs all actions, as per its wish. Let me take an example of the film (movie) industry, where director is the most important person. Director is the central point of control and exercises this allocated authority by calling the shots, literally, in this example.

All other contributors, in their individual capacity are very important and many a time their contributions are crucial to the scheme of things, but the person who carries the onus of final delivery, is the director. This burden gives the director, an absolute control and unquestioned power over all the other contributors and also the undisputed authority over defining factors and process parameters, which give shape to the final product. Similarly, the mind is responsible for our well-being and also provides for all other issues like desires, wants and realization of our dreams, which are the targeted results. This responsibility also gives the mind complete authority over all the other parts of the whole.

Another example that the young and old both may find that they can relate to easily, is about slimming, or addressing obesity issues.

Please try to eat five small meals instead of 3 big meals. Frequent food inputs give a signal to the mind that availability of food is not an issue at all.

So, our mind, which controls the body, promotes active lifestyle, which will, as an obvious consequence, address obesity issues by encouraging increase of the base metabolic rate (BMR). This directly translates to enabling of the higher energy spending, thereby addressing obesity.

However, if we resort to skipping a meal, in our quest for reducing body weight and volume, a pseudo-logical step of reducing the input to curb the storage of fat, to achieve slimming targets; the mind gets a derived input that famine is about to strike and embarks upon the process of storing energy for future use, when this accumulation may be needed to sustain life. Our body stores energy in the form of fat accumulation. This also translates to another problem that the mind actively engages in slowing down all body processes.

The basic purpose of slowing down of all body processes is to reduce energy expenditure, thereby conserving energy. Not only we become more obese, we also feel lethargic, as the mind starts operating in base survival mode and rations energy spending based on the result of internal energy audit, which in this scenario, recommends aggregation to provide for future needs.

A word of caution is needed here. It is to be ensured that the total food intake in five meals is less than the current total food intake amount in three meals put together. Another requirement is that we must succeed in our attempt to tempt the mind into physical activity by providing such options as have been known to be found interesting in the past by our mind.

We may also need to use deceptive coercive measures, such as telling the brain that a cricket, soccer and/ or tennis video transmission or a video game, incorporating these sports will be enjoyed much more by us, when we have played the actual game and understand the finer issues. Please note that this ploy of our mind working out an incentive, to be presented to self, may not always work.

After all, who are we trying to fool? I may not be as gullible as I may think and would surely work out the stratagem. The underlying belief, on which we base our subterfuge, is that our mind wants to take care of our well-being and will readily allow an option to be accepted, if the proposed option aims to benefit us, even if an excuse is used.

I may actually be forgiven by my mind for trying to bring in a coerced lifestyle change that is an assured benefit and the mind may actually go along with my scheming agenda that attempts to influence it to choose an active lifestyle and make healthy food choices, which are beneficial for the body, in which the mind resides and are targeted towards achieving a healthy lifestyle that ensures continuation of healthy life for the body in long term perspective.

The care to be exercised in this effort is that, these outdoor undertakings should be kept within short manageable duration to begin with, so that these do not tax us too much and put us off the endeavor.

Now that we have lured the mind outside, all we need to do is to keep our mind interested by introducing variations that are akin to an interesting new feature addition to the video game liked by us.

The attempt now is to keep us outside, even with guile, if required. All of this is aimed at changing the sedentary lifestyle to a regular energetic one that helps to increase our daily energy expenditure, which directly addresses obesity issues.

The involved issue here is that when we try to cheat our own mind, the mind already knows all about this attempt to fool it. How are we going to succeed then? Who is fooling whom? When I find myself on both sides of the equation, this becomes an untenable proposition.

If the fact be known, nobody is getting fooled as this ruse is recognized much before it is implemented. The primary goal and thought of the mind is to keep the body healthy. There is nothing virtuous about it also.

This indeed is a purely selfish thought aimed at self-preservation, as the survival of the mind is directly linked to that of the body in which it resides.

The basic instinct of the mind beyond preservation of self and perpetuation of the race and family line is the need for saving sufficient means to provide for energy expenditure, as and when required.

In this thinking mode, our mind operates in a manner akin to the respected homemakers, who, being without an independent source of income, tend to become compulsive hoarders.

The mind also tends to store energy and releases only enough for the current needs, in this operational mode of thinking. This propensity of the mind gives it a natural orientation of being lethargic and a work shirker. The physical manifestation of this thought gets us in to the mode of lethargic stupor and we are labeled 'lazy bones'. How come not everyone is found just lazing around? After-all, the minds, all of them, at least in this scenario, work with the same logic and should also follow the same directed action pattern.

The distinguishing element is that, some of us show our minds by example and in literal terms that, if we invest some energy now, this energy spending for lively endeavors, will help us in acquiring additional ability to procure more food, which is raw input for energy that helps us to acquire greater ability of perpetuating the race and our own lineage.

Energy audit has been established to be a major influence for the mind and body in terms of availability or scarcity of this much valued resource.

The main issue here is that, once convinced of the ability of energetic endeavor to satisfy basic needs, the mind is fully willing to spend energy and the only issue is that the inertia, which holds us captive, must be manipulated in an effective manner to lend its weight to momentum, to achieve all that is our purpose and also the targeted objective.

The other issue is that no one wants to chart a new course as a new path may be fraught with problems and even dangers that we may not have the ability to think of, acknowledge and understand, at this time.

We need a pioneer, every time we attempt a course of action not traversed, as yet. This pioneer has to be imbued with the ability to traverse the uncharted route and an uncertain itinerary with confidence.

Each and every age has had their pioneers and it is only now that cocooned in the environment of easy availability of all the pleasant amenities of life, all our basic needs of survival and security satisfied, in this era of plenty; when we look out and even plan for something radical, we tend to look for safe radical endeavors and this safe orientation and resultant safe classification renders the radical tag of the endeavor, both ineffective and inconsequential.

Now, we feel empowered enough to undertake discussion on the topic of resolution and dissolution. A resolution is made up of several thoughts that are analogous, yet retain their distinctive thought form to enable this resolution to acquire a characteristic configuration that defines finer nuances of the thought form, which gives the resolution its characteristic manifestation and distinguishing expression.

The dissolution must not be misconstrued to mean annihilation of the thought. Dissolution is to be thought of as elimination of the ideas that are inimical to immediate context in particular and the overall doctrine in general.

This existing framework is populated with residual ideas that have passed the test of time and have proven their relevance to the context. This partly populated framework can now be used in alignment with the new entrants to the domain for another thought construct.

Risk and errors:

Why do we take a risk?

What makes us commit errors?

Within our own group, we cannot hide behind the facade of the proclamation, "We are only human and hence prone to errors." We need to look at the root cause of the action orientation in this perspective.

We tend to attempt a risky endeavor even with an associated loss probability, if the potential benefits are tempting enough. In the Wimbledon live telecast, I saw one of the players trying to hit the ball in such a manner, so as to ensure that the ball lands very close to the sidelines, so that the opponent may fail to reach it and thereby concede a point. There is a distinct probability that the ball may land beyond the sideline but our brain weighs and decides the potential benefit to be worth taking the risk, even when the loss probability is high and this may actually result in an unforced error and the resultant loss of a point.

We tend to avoid risk to mitigate the consequence of a loss but court the risk when there is even a remote chance of a cognizable potential benefit.

Who is the one, who makes the sun set and then rise again in eternal celebration of another sparkling new day?

Who sends the waves to the seashore, in a continual spectacle of confrontation of might of the sea and forbearance of the seashore?

Tolerance of the seashore is its strength and may not be thought of as meek compliance of the submissive shore, to the might of the ocean.

Who decides as to when the flow of air is a pleasant breeze and when it becomes the destructive force of a tornado?

The omnipotent, the omnipresent and the omniscient, I seek thee, let me come to you.

"Come, my child and rest with me. You are a peaceful soul."

Glossary:

Adolf Hitler: Austrian-born German politician and the leader of the National Socialist German Workers Party. He was chancellor of Germany from 1933 to 1945 and dictator of Nazi Germany (as Führer and Reichskanzler) from 1934 to 1945. Hitler was at the center of the founding of Nazism, the start of World War II, and the Holocaust.

Abraham Lincoln: Abraham Lincoln, the 16th President of the United States successfully led his country through its greatest constitutional, military and moral crisis – the American Civil War – preserving the Union while ending slavery, and promoting economic and financial modernization.

Albert Einstein: Albert Einstein was a German theoretical physicist, who developed the theory of general relativity, affecting a revolution in physics. For this achievement, Einstein is often regarded as the father of modern physics. Einstein is generally considered to be the most influential physicist of the 20th century.

Amitabh Bachchan: Amitabh Bachchan is an Indian film Icon. He first gained popularity in the early 1970s as the "angry young man" of Hindi cinema, and has since appeared in over 180 Indian films in a career spanning more than four decades. Amitabh Bachchan is regarded as one of the greatest and most influential actors in the history of Indian cinema.

Beatles: The Beatles were an English rock band formed in Liverpool in 1960 and one of the most commercially successful and critically acclaimed acts in the history of popular music.

Bertrand Russell: British philosopher, logician, mathematician, historian, and social critic.

Chanakya: Chanakya was an Indian teacher, philosopher and royal adviser. Originally a teacher at the ancient Takshashila University, Chanakya was the architect of the first Maurya Emperor Chandragupta's rise to power at a young age. He is widely credited for having played an important role in the establishment of the Maurya Empire.

Chow kok koh: Chow kok koh or Zhang Guo Lao is one of the famed Eight Immortals of the Chinese mythology and one of the most eccentric deities.

Clarence Darrow: was an American lawyer and leading member of the American Civil Liberties Union.

Darwin: Charles Robert Darwin, FRS (12February 1809–19April 1882) was an English naturalist. He established that all species of life have descended over time from common ancestors, and proposed the scientific theory that this branching pattern of evolution resulted from a process that he called natural selection and the theory of 'survival of the fittest'.

Elvis Presley: Elvis Aaron Presley was one of the most popular American singers of the 20th century. A cultural icon, he is widely known by the single name Elvis. He is often referred to as the "King of Rock and Roll" or simply "the King".

Gandhi: Indian freedom fighter, proponent of Ahimsa (non-violence), the principal leader of India's independence movement and the Father of the Nation.

George Bernard Shaw: An Irish playwright, philosopher and a co-founder of the London School of Economics.

Herm Albright: Painter, lithographer, born on Jan. 29, 1876 in Mannheim, Germany. Herm *Albright studied music and philosophy at the Heidelberg University*

IT: Information Technology

Jawaharlal Nehru: first Prime Minister of independent India (1947–64) and one of the principle founders of the Non-Aligned Movement. He was one of the principal leaders of India's independence movement.

<u>Jennifer Lopez</u>: Jennifer Lynn Lopez is an American actress, businesswoman, dancer and recording artist; often referred to as J. Lo. She is reportedly the highest earning actress of Latin American descent.

<u>John F. Kennedy</u>: John Fitzgerald "Jack" Kennedy, often referred to by his initials JFK, was the <u>35th President of the United States</u>, serving from 1961 until his assassination in 1963.

<u>Lenin Vladimir</u>: Vladimir Ilyich Lenin was a <u>Russian Marxist</u> <u>revolutionary</u>, intellectual and politician who led the <u>October Revolution of 1917</u>. As leader of the <u>Bolsheviks</u>, he headed the <u>Soviet</u> state during its initial years (1917–1924), as it fought to establish control of Russia in the <u>Russian Civil War</u> and worked to create a socialist economic system.

<u>Locke</u>: John Locke, widely known as the *Father of classical liberalism,* was an English philosopher and physician regarded as one of the most influential of Enlightenment thinkers.

<u>Madonna</u>: Madonna is an American singer-song writer, dancer, and actress. She has sold 300 to 500 million records worldwide.

<u>Mao Zedong</u>: Mao Zedong, also transliterated as Mao Tse-tung, and commonly referred to as Chairman Mao was a <u>Chinese</u> <u>Communist</u> <u>revolutionary</u>, <u>guerrilla warfare</u> strategist, <u>Marxist</u> <u>political philosopher</u>, and leader of the <u>Chinese Revolution</u>. He was the architect and <u>founding father</u> of the <u>People's Republic of China</u>.

<u>Mark Twain</u>: American author and humorist.

<u>Paris Hilton</u>: Paris Whitney Hilton (born February 17, 1981) is an American businesswoman, a potential heiress, producer and socialite.

Patton George S: George Smith Patton, Jr. was an <u>officer</u> in the <u>United States Army</u>, best known for his leadership as a <u>general</u> during <u>World War II</u>.

RAM: Random Access Memory is a semiconductor based computer memory with fast access time. The organization of the RAM is based on the algorithm that uses the most accessed and most recently accessed information tags for its organization and operation.

ROM: *Read Only Memory. Information is written once only in the ROM.*

Rommel: Erwin Johannes Eugen Rommel, popularly known as the Desert Fox, was a German Field Marshal of World War II. He won the respect of both his own troops and also the enemies he fought.

Sigmund Freud: Sigmund Freud was a Jewish neurologist who founded the discipline of psychoanalysis.

Thomas Edison: Thomas Alva Edison was an American inventor and businessman. He developed many devices that greatly influenced the life around the world, including the phonograph, the motion picture camera, and a long-lasting, practical electric light bulb.

Winston Churchill: British Conservative politician and statesman known for his leadership of the United Kingdom during the Second World War. Widely regarded as one of the greatest wartime leaders of the century, he served as Prime Minister twice (1940–45 and 1951–55). A noted statesman and orator, Churchill was also an officer in the British Army, a historian, a writer, and an artist. He was the first person to be made an honorary citizen of the United States of America.

Yoga-nidra: Yoga-nidra or 'yogic sleep' is a sleep-like trance state which yogis report to experience during their meditations. The practice of yoga relaxation has been found to reduce tension and anxiety.

Bibliography:

The Plague – Albert Camus

Man and Superman – George Bernard Shaw

Unpopular essays – Bertrand Russell

Ancient Hindu philosophy chronicles

Buddhist philosophy chronicles

Panchtantra stories

Jatak katha

Magazines:

Reader's Digest

India Today

-------------------------------|||--------------------------

email: rohit.agnihotri@cmcltd.com

Alternate email: ragnihotri@yahoo.com